The Malaysian Banking Industry

The book provides students and academics in finance and banking with the most recent updates and changes in the Malaysian banking sector post-AFC period. The book explores the evolution of banking policies and practices after the "Tomyam Goong" crisis and investigates the health of Malaysian banks via efficiency measurement. In addition, it also presents the evolution of bank risk management regulations and practices in Malaysia. The book also discusses the effectiveness of the Malaysian bank bailout strategy with comparison to the banks' bailout in developed countries such as the US.

This book is important and timely since there are very limited books in the market that cover the recent developments on Malaysian banking sectors in the post-AFC period. Hence, this book serves as a valuable resource for all finance and banking students, academic researchers, and practitioners not limited to the Asian region that require in-depth insights on the latest policies and practices in the Malaysian banking sector.

Rozaimah Zainudin is Senior Lecturer at the Faculty of Business and Accountancy, University of Malaya, Malaysia. Prior to joining academia, she worked in the banking sector for seven years and was attached to a Banking Operations and System Department. Her areas of research include risk management, derivative markets, corporate finance, and international finance. Her research projects currently involve banking and financial wellbeing.

Chan Sok-Gee is Senior Lecturer at the Faculty of Business and Accountancy, University of Malaya, Malaysia. Her commitment to research and publication, especially on the topic of bank performance, has led to her publication in world-recognized journals, such as the *Global Economic Review, Review of Managerial Science, Prague Economic Papers*, and others. Besides bank performance, her research areas include corporate governance and bank efficiency, economic efficiency analysis, and value-added tax. She has also been recognized as an outstanding young researcher by the University of Malaya. She serves as Editor-in-Chief of the *Asian Journal of Economics, Business and Accounting.*

Aidil Rizal Shahrin is Senior Lecturer at the Department of Banking and Finance, Faculty of Business and Accountancy, University of Malaya, Malaysia. His research focuses on applied econometrics in the areas of finance and macroeconomics. He has been published in internationally refereed journals, such as the *Journal of Economics and Statistics*, the *Romanian Journal of Forecasting*, and the *International Journal of Statistics and Economics*. Recently, he has focused on bank efficiency, emphasizing the econometrics methodology.

Routledge Focus on Economics and Finance

The fields of economics are constantly expanding and evolving. This growth presents challenges for readers trying to keep up with the latest important insights. Routledge Focus on Economics and Finance presents short books on the latest big topics, linking in with the most cutting-edge economics research.

Individually, each title in the series provides coverage of a key academic topic, whilst collectively the series forms a comprehensive collection across the whole spectrum of economics.

The Essentials of M&A Due Diligence
Peter Howson

Cities, Economic Inequality and Justice
Reflections and Alternative Perspectives
Edwin Buitelaar, Anet Weterings and Roderik Ponds

Reinventing Accounting and Finance Education
For a Caring, Inclusive and Sustainable Planet
Atul Shah

Microfinance
Research, Debates, Policy
Bernd Balkenhol

The Malaysian Banking Industry
Policies and Practices after the Asian Financial Crisis
Rozaimah Zainudin, Chan Sok-Gee, and Aidil Rizal Shahrin

For a full list of titles in this series, please visit www.routledge.com/Routledge-Focus-on-Economics-and-Finance/book-series/RFEF

The Malaysian Banking Industry

Policies and Practices after the Asian Financial Crisis

Rozaimah Zainudin, Chan Sok-Gee, and Aidil Rizal Shahrin

Routledge
Taylor & Francis Group
LONDON AND NEW YORK

First published 2019
by Routledge
2 Park Square, Milton Park, Abingdon, Oxon OX14 4RN

and by Routledge
711 Third Avenue, New York, NY 10017

Routledge is an imprint of the Taylor & Francis Group, an informa business

British Library Cataloguing-in-Publication Data
A catalogue record for this book is available from the British Library

Library of Congress Cataloging-in-Publication Data
Names: Zainudin, Rozaimah, 1974– author. | Gee, Chan Sok, 1979– author. | Shahrin, Aidil Rizal, 1977– author.
Title: The Malaysian banking industry policies and practices after the Asian financial crisis / by Rozaimah Zainudin, Chan Sok Gee and Aidil Rizal Shahrin.
Description: First Edition. | New York : Routledge, 2019. | Series: Routledge focus on economics and finance | Includes bibliographical references and index.
Identifiers: LCCN 2018018340 | ISBN 9781138545779 (hardback) | ISBN 9781351000512 (ebook)
Subjects: LCSH: Banks and banking—Malaysia. | Financial institutions—Malaysia.
Classification: LCC HG3300.6.A6 Z345 2019 | DDC 332.109595—dc23
LC record available at https://lccn.loc.gov/2018018340

ISBN: 978-1-138-54577-9 (hbk)
ISBN: 978-1-351-00051-2 (ebk)

Typeset in Times New Roman
by Apex CoVantage, LLC

Contents

Figures

Tables

Preface

A sound and resilient banking industry has always been the main interest and objective of the banking authorities, and has been widely studied by both practitioners and academics. This is because the occurrences of banking crisis drastically affect, if not cripple, an economy. This was seen during the collapse of the banking industry in Asia during the 1997 Asian financial crisis (AFC) and in developed economies during the 2008 global financial crisis (GFC).

Major banking consolidation and reregulation took place in the Asian region. Malaysia was no exception, taking different strategies in the banking consolidation and reregulation process, for which it received both positive feedback and also criticism from the rest of the world. The exercises initiated by the Malaysian government and banking authorities effectively rationalized and consolidated 94% of the domestic banking industry's assets in a move to protect the banking industry from the negative effects of the Asian financial crisis. Nevertheless, the efficiency of the banking industry following banking consolidation and reregulation has yet to produce conclusive outcomes. There are also not many comprehensive studies of developments in the Malaysian banking industry. The main objective of this volume is thus to provide information on the evolution of and changes in the Malaysian banking sector landscape following the Asian financial crisis period.

Additionally, bank bailout has been a popular response to banking crisis in both developed and developing countries. The 2008 global financial crisis also resulted in a bank bailout in the developed countries of Europe and the US. Yet there is no conclusive evidence regarding the role of bank bailouts in either developed or developing countries that could be used to support or criticize the actions of the local authorities. Furthermore, such bailout policies are often blamed for moral hazard behaviour in the banking industry. We therefore seek to contribute to the literature on the role of bailouts in banks' moral hazard behaviour. To do so, we compare the various bailout programs that have been implemented in developed and developing countries, with the aim of evaluating their success or failure. We select Malaysia to represent a developing country and the US to represent a developed country, and compare them in terms of the differences and similarities of their bailout programs and their effectiveness. This study is thus expected to contribute to the wider perspective on the effectiveness of bailout programs around the world. It also provides policy implications for future bank bailout programs through evaluating the factors that contribute to the success and failure of bank bailouts by the local authorities. Hence, our book is intended to cater to a wide range of readers: students, researchers, practitioners, policy makers, and all who are keen to know more about the Malaysian banking industry.

This book is divided into three major parts, aimed at:

i) evaluating the overall health of the banking industry in Malaysia through bank efficiency analyses;
ii) studying the risk management function of banks in Malaysia in terms of its evolution and its future key challenges;
iii) to examine the effectiveness of bank bailouts in Malaysia as compared with those in a developed country.

The book can be used a reference for undergraduate and postgraduate courses including bank management, money and banking, treasury management, and Islamic banking studies. As part of that, the book can also be employed to enhance the understanding of practitioners or academics examining the many changes that occurred in the Malaysian banking sectors' landscape after the AFC period. Finally, the authors hope that readers be able to benefit and find the contents useful in enhancing their understanding of the updates in the Malaysian banking sectors since the AFC period.

Our special thanks go to the Equitable Society Research Cluster University of Malaya Research Grant (RP037–16SBS), which supported our research and publication. Without such support, this book would not have been completed. We further thank our families and friends, who provided us with much support in the success of the book.

Rozaimah Zainudin, Chan Sok-Gee, and Aidil Rizal Shahrin
Department of Finance and Banking
Faculty of Business and Accountancy
University of Malaya
Kuala Lumpur, Malaysia
2018

Abbreviations

ABIF	ASEAN Banking Integration Framework
AFC	Asian financial crisis
AGP	Asset Guarantee Program
AMC	Asset management companies
API	Application programming interface
ASEAN	Association of Southeast Asian Nations
BBA	*Bai' bithaman ajil*
BNM	Bank Negara Malaysia
CAFIB	Capital Adequacy Framework for Islamic Banking Institutions
CAP	Capital Assistance Program
CCM	Companies Commission of Malaysia
CCR	Core capital ratio
CDFI	Community Development Financial Institution
CDO	Collateralized debt obligations
CDRC	Corporate Debt Restructuring Committee
CEO	Chief Executive Officer
CMM	Continuous model monitoring
COSO	Committee of Sponsoring Organizations of the Treadway Commission
CPP	Capital Purchase Program
CRO	Chief Risk Officer
DB	Deutsche Bank
DEA	Data envelopment analysis
DMU	Decision Making Units
ECF	Equity crowdfunding platform
EESA	Emergency Economic Stabilization Act
EPF	Employment Provident Fund
FAOM	Fintech Association of Malaysia
FDIC	Federal Deposit Insurance Corporation
FRMC	Financial Risk Management Committee

FSI	Financial soundness indicators
FSMP	I Financial Sector Master Plan I
FSMP	II Financial Sector Master Plan II
GARP	Global Association of Risk Professionals
GDP	Gross domestic product
GFC	Global financial crisis
GST	Goods and Services Tax
IBFIM	Islamic Banking and Finance Institute Malaysia
IBS	Islamic banking institutions
IMF	International Monetary Fund
JPMC	JPMorgan Chase
LCR	Liquidity coverage ratio
LR	Liquidity ratio
LtoA	Liquid assets to total assets
LtoSTL	Liquid assets to short-term liabilities
MaGIC	Malaysian Global Innovation & Creativity Centre
MDEC	Malaysian Digital Economy Corporation
MRCAF	Market Risk-Capital Adequacy Framework
NEAC	National Economic Action Council
NERP	National Economy Recovery Plan
NPL	Nonperforming loan
NSFR	Net stable funding ratio
PRMIA	Professional Risk Managers' International Association
RMA	Risk Management Association
RMC	Risk Management Committee
RMU	Risk Management Unit
ROA	Return on asset
ROE	Return on equity
RWCR	Risk weighted capital ratio
SCAP	Supervisory Capital Assessment Program
SFA	Stochastic Frontier Analysis
SME	Small and medium enterprise
SPV	Special purpose vehicles
TAF	Term Auction Facility
TARP	Troubled Asset Relief Program
TIP	Targeted Investment Program
TRMS	Treasury Risk Management Section
UK	United Kingdom
US	United States

1 The Malaysian banking industry

Policies and practices after the Asian financial crisis

Rozaimah Zainudin and Chan Sok-Gee

1.1 The banking sector landscape since the Asian financial crisis

The health of the banking industry has always been of concern to both regulators and researchers alike. This is because banking industry failures have drastic, if not crippling, effects on the economy. This was evident during the 1997 Asian financial crisis (AFC) and the 2008 global financial crisis (GFC), where bank runs led to the impairment of the economies in developing and developed countries. It is crucial for banking sector sustainability to be capable of absorbing very high levels of unpredictable economic shock. Crises generally appear with many signals, but the questions are how the economy can detect the warning signals and how strong each country's banking sectors needs to be to absorb the shock. This is crucial because banking failure leads to impairment in the payment system that distorts economic growth in the long run.

In context of Malaysia, the AFC demonstrated the fragility of domestic banks to the external shock that moved contagiously from the other ASEAN countries. The AFC challenged the Malaysian banking sector's financial performance and its soundness as the medium of financial intermediation within the Malaysian economy. During the crisis, the Malaysian government, along with the national central bank, Bank Negara Malaysia (BNM), aggressively introduced various monetary and fiscal policies to strengthen the financial system, and especially the operation of banking institutions. The banking sector reform policies were implemented to boost public and external confidence in the role of the banks as lending and deposit-taking institutions during the crisis period. Since the AFC period, these measures have acted as precautions against potentially enormous systematic risk in the banking sector (BNM, 1999). Amongst the measures taken were:

i) bank consolidation exercises among the financial institutions;
ii) the introduction of Danaharta as the national asset management organization responsible for the excess of nonperforming loans (NPLs) that arose during the AFC period;
iii) the establishment of Danamodal to act as the special purpose vehicle to rescue financial institutions that faced capital shortage;
iv) the setting up of a Corporate Debt Restructuring Committee to rescue large companies that faced extreme debt problems, as such problems in larger corporations would cause the negative effects to spill over and to increase the already high levels of NPLs held by the banks.

Most countries in South East Asia were affected by the AFC and resorted to major bank consolidation and reregulation processes as part of a bank bailout policy. Such actions were initiated by the national governments or by the International Monetary Fund (IMF). Unlike other countries in Asia, the Malaysian authority opted not to accept any bailout from the IMF, instead implementing various in-house policies – including forced mergers – to improve the performance of Malaysian banks and to strengthen their positions, in order to withstand future economic shocks. In Malaysia, the 1997 AFC severely affected the solvency of the banking industry, leading to a major consolidation of the industry through forced mergers by BNM, as well as capital injections. By 31 December 2000, 50 out of 54 locally owned banking institutions in Malaysia had been consolidated into ten banking groups. This exercise effectively rationalized and consolidated 94% of the total assets of the domestic banking industry in Malaysia, in order to protect the banking industry from the negative effects of the financial crisis.

Apart from bank consolidation, BNM also implemented various measurements to improve the weak risk management controls of banks. These included recapitalization and restructuring of the banking industry for a more resilient and sound financial system. The dearth of bank risk management further contributed to the mismatch between the Malaysian banks' risk profile and the minimum capital controls imposed by BNM. This gap resulted in overstated bank levels of capital, and hence an inability to absorb the large shock of the AFC (BNM Annual Report, 1999). Since the AFC period, the central bank has thus revisited the capital adequacy framework to ensure that the real bank risk profiles are commensurate with strengthening bank risk management practices. A revised risk management framework was thus introduced:

> *to enable identification, quantification, monitoring, and management of all associated risks. The risk management framework must also be flexible and sophisticated to accommodate for changes in the electronic environment and advancements in technology.*
>
> (BNM Annual Report, 2000, p. 5)

In addition, the implementation of the Malaysia Deposit Insurance System in 2011, the revision of the Corporate Governance Code of Conduct since 2000, and the adoption of Basel III requirements after the GFC were undertaken to improve the risk-taking aspects of the domestic banking industry in Malaysia. These measures were meant to further strengthen the banking industry and safeguard depositors, while building a sustainable payment system that would contribute to the economic growth of the country.

Many studies have presented empirical evidence of bank performance measurements, risk-taking issues, liquidity issues, and others. These have focused in different ways on bank-related issues, and the results are not conclusive. Furthermore, comprehensive studies are relatively scant for the Malaysian banking industry's developments, especially in terms of policies and practices in the aftermath of the AFC. Studies of the Malaysian banking industry are important in providing a proof of success and a checklist to banking authorities in terms of the banking consolidation and reregulation, which in this country involved different strategies in the bailout policy. This book thus sheds light on the effectiveness and efficacy of the bailout policy implemented in Malaysia, which could serve as a model to both developing and developed economies. The goal of this book is threefold: First, it provides a comprehensive evaluation of the policies and practices of the Malaysian banking industry since the AFC in context of both general and Islamic banking institutions. We focus on the management and allocation of banking resources by studying the efficiency level of the banks. In this context, we measure the profit, cost, and technical efficiency of these Malaysian banks by comparing conventional and Islamic banks. Second, this book examines the effect of risk-taking activities, policies, and practices at Malaysian banks after the AFC period. Third, it considers how initiation of bank consolidation in Malaysia was meant to strengthen the financial system, which was crucial because bank bailout policy had been widely questioned as it creates excessive risk-taking, defeating the main objective of creating sound, healthy financial institutions through consolidation, as the evidence from the US suggests. This book also evaluates the effectiveness of banking consolidation in Malaysia by looking at banks' efficiency levels before and after the consolidation exercise. The book also attempts to evaluate the effectiveness of the US bank bailout programs in the GFC period. In a nutshell, this volume aims to shed light on the post-AFC occurrences in the Malaysian banking industry landscape, encompassing the health of the banking industry, bank risk management practices, and the effectiveness of the bank consolidation and bailout strategy in terms of overall bank efficiency. Apart from the domestic analysis, the book compares the best risk management practices and the effectiveness of the bank bailout policies implemented by Malaysian and US banks.

1.2 Contents and organization

This book contains five chapters, summarized as follows:

Chapter 1: The Malaysian Banking Industry: Policies and Practices after the Asian Financial Crisis

Chapter 1 gives an overview of how the Malaysian banking landscape has changed since the AFC period. This chapter further discusses the major changes in the Malaysian banking sector according to three perspectives; namely, bank efficiency, risk-management regulations and practices, and the bank consolidation programme after the AFC crisis.

Chapter 2: The Health of the Malaysian Banking Industry

This chapter presents a comprehensive review of the bank practices in Malaysia since the Asian financial crisis, describing first the general changes in the Malaysian banking landscape, and then proceeding to discuss the changes within Islamic banking institutions. The chapter provides a detailed evaluation of the overall health of the Malaysian banking industry through bank efficiency analyses, involving aspects such as the bank's allocation of resources through technical efficiency, cost efficiency, and profit efficiency. This is crucial as it deals with the management of bank resources to achieve maximum output while fulfilling the objectives of cost minimization and profit maximization. The chapter then compares the levels of efficiency of conventional and Islamic banks in Malaysia.

Chapter 3: Bank Risk Management

This chapter describes the evolution of the risk management function of banks in Malaysia and continues to evaluate the Malaysian banking industry's resilience by studying the evolution of this risk management regulations implemented by BNM. It compares the current local situation with that of global best practices. The chapter also identifies the likely future challenges to be faced by the risk management function. This enables us to gauge the effectiveness of the Malaysian banking industry's risk management practices and provides some insight to policy makers and bank managers, which they can use to develop better strategies for a healthy banking industry.

Chapter 4: Bank Bailout Efficacy

Chapter 4 explains the concept of moral hazard theory and relates it to bank consolidation policy. It provides a detailed review of the Malaysian context before, during, and after the AFC period. Next, the chapter evaluates the effects on the overall Malaysian bank efficiency of the bank consolidation and forced merger exercises after the AFC period. A comprehensive review is then given of the bank bailout experience at US banks before, during, and after the GFC period. In this chapter, we further compare the bank bailout strategy implemented at US banks after the GFC period.

Chapter 5: Conclusion

This chapter concludes the empirical evidence from Chapters 2, 3, and 4. The chapter also provides a few practical suggestions for BNM regulators and bankers to further improve banking sector performance and remain competitive globally.

Chapter 6: Special Topic: Practitioner Insight on Risk-Management Practices

This special topic provides a review of Malaysian risk-management practices from the perspective of a practitioner. The chapter discusses the best practices of risk-management using JPMorgan Chase and Deutsche Bank as examples. Finally, the chapter presents the future challenges for the overall banking industry.

References

Bank Negara Malaysia. (1999). *The Central Bank and the Financial System in Malaysia: A Decade of Change (1989–1999)*. Kuala Lumpur: Bank Negara Malaysia.

Bank Negara Malaysia Annual Report 1999. Retrieved from http://www.bnm.gov.my/index.php?ch=en_publication&pg=en_ar&ac=3&lang=en

Bank Negara Malaysia Annual Report 2000. Retrieved from http://www.bnm.gov.my/index.php?ch=en_publication&pg=en_ar&ac=3&lang=en

2 The health of the Malaysian banking industry

Rozaimah Zainudin and Chan Sok-Gee

2.1 Overview

The Malaysian central bank, Bank Negara Malaysia (BNM), began operations on 26 January 1959 with the aim of providing the basic infrastructure of the Malaysian financial system and strengthening domestic commercial banks in the economy. A decade later, BNM began to encourage the establishment of other forms of financial intermediaries, such as investment banks (merchant banks) and financial institutions offering types of services other than those offered by the domestic commercial banks. These financial intermediaries provide a broader variety of business and consumer financing products to the Malaysian financial market.

The main function of BNM is to improve monetary and financial stability through monetary policy. It is crucial to provide the Malaysian economy with conducive and sustainable growth through the correct implementation of monetary policy. This is because the right monetary policy is useful for price stability, and hence the overall stability of the financial system.

BNM also implements various strategies to deepen and strengthen financial markets and the foreign exchange market. This can be seen in the active role BNM has played in stabilizing the financial system, especially during the economic crises of the past decades. In the1980s, BNM implemented many measures to strengthen the regulatory and supervisory framework with the aim of stabilizing the financial and monetary market during the commodity crisis of the early 1980s, as well as the electronics crisis of 1985. As a result, these crises did not directly affect the banking system in Malaysia.

During 1997, the Malaysian economy was greatly affected by the Asian financial crisis (AFC), due to the contagion effect of the slump in foreign exchange rates from Thailand. This led to a major change in the landscape of banking. The change in the landscape was due not only to the effects of the AFC, but also to changes in banking technology. Domestic financial institutions were forced to keep up with these changes and absorbed financial liberalization via borderless financial services. These technology changes and financial liberalization induced competition among local banking institutions. Apart from technology change, AFC was another crisis to be remembered in the Malaysian banking industry. From 1997 to 1998, the industry was greatly affected by a sharp increase in the ratio of nonperforming loans to gross loans, from 4.06% to 18.60%. This resulted in bank runs and required major restructuring and recapitalization of the banking industry as a whole. The crisis served as a warning to BNM regarding its primary role in promoting prudent banking. However, even a prudent banking system might not have absorbed the shock created during the AFC. The AFC was another significant milestone in the BNM's realization of the fragility of Malaysian banking institutions during that period. Another major reformation to strengthen banking regulations and operations therefore took place after the AFC. The ratio of nonperforming to total loans began to drop in 2002, following the steps taken by BNM to strengthen banking regulations and operations. Thanks to the improved prudential supervisory function of BNM, the Malaysian banking industry was not strongly affected by the global financial crisis (GFC) of the mid-2000s. This can be seen from the ratio of nonperforming loans to gross loans, which continued to decrease from 2008 to 2015, as shown in Figure 2.1.

Remarkable changes have occurred in the Malaysian banking landscape since the AFC, especially with BNM's introduction of the merger program, which was initiated to strengthen those banking institutions in Malaysia that had been badly hit during the AFC. Furthermore, the merger program

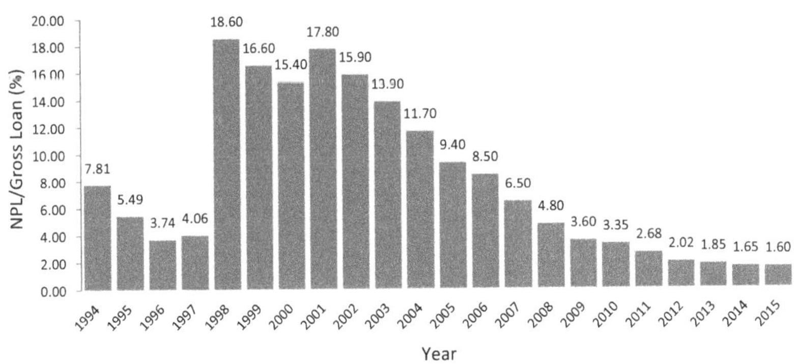

Figure 2.1 Nonperforming loans as a percentage of gross loans

Source: Monthly Statistical Bulletin: Various Issues and Global Financial Development Dataset, the World Bank

is said to have further increased the scale of operations of the banks, by increasing their size through consolidation. Banks are expected to reap gains from economies of scale after the merger process. This is supported by Yudistira (2004), who indicates that bank mergers allow institutions to expand horizontally through the greater acquisition of assets that contribute to more efficient banking operations via economies of scale. Banking consolidation also aims to reform domestic banking structures to increase the ability of local banks to absorb the unpredictable external shocks of crises.

The merger program proposed that ten anchor banks undergo forced merger with 54 other financial institutions. In 1998, structural reforms were undertaken by the banking sector to ensure the local banking sector could adapt and cope with further adverse economic events and future shocks (BNM Annual Report, 1998, 1999). A comprehensive discussion on the Malaysian bank consolidation exercise after the AFC period is presented in Chapter 4. The consolidation aimed to increase the effectiveness and efficiency of domestic banks in order to compete in the more intense business environment, which is expected to be more integrated as a result of advances in technology and trade integration. The flow of the merger program is illustrated in Figure 2.2.

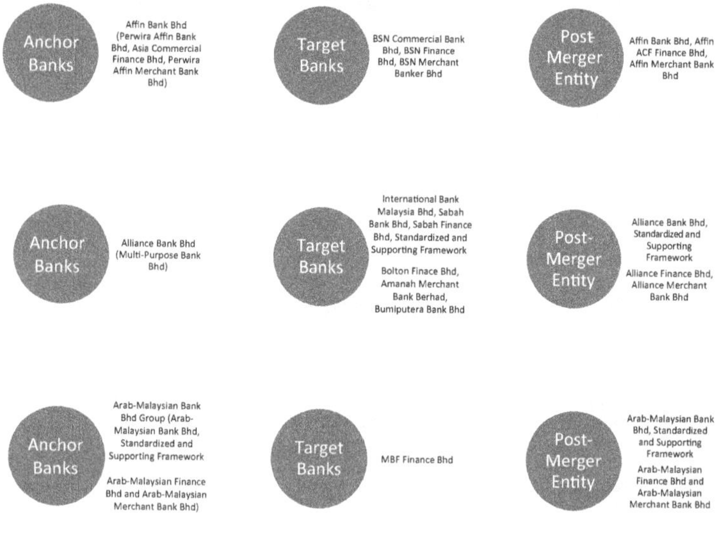

Figure 2.2 Merger program for Malaysian banks

Source: BNM Annual Report (2001, p. 111)

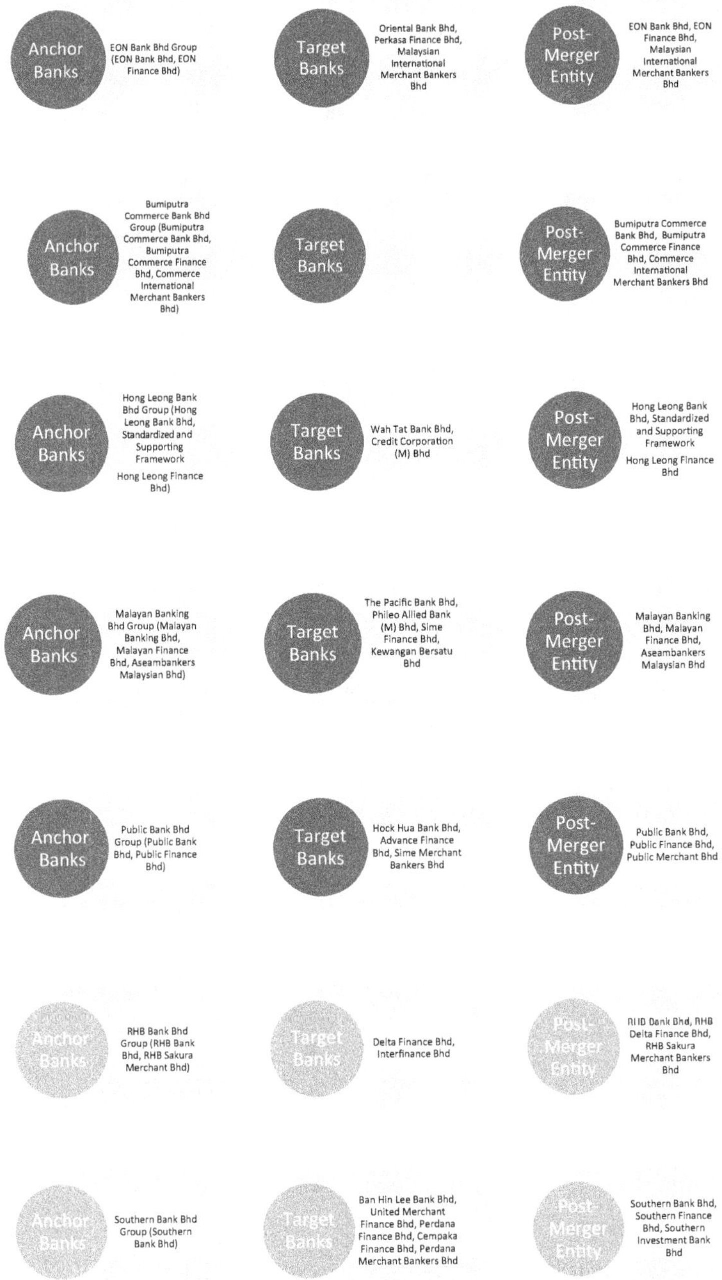

Figure 2.2 (Continued)

2.1.1 Banking sector performance

The banking industry in Malaysia has been growing steadily since the establishment of the banking infrastructure in the country in the 1960s. This can be seen from Figure 2.2, which shows that the private credit of domestic banks has grown since 1960. We can see that, even starting from 1981, the ratio of private credit to GDP in Malaysia reached 52.58%, comprising half of all economic activity in Malaysia. This indicates the significance of the banking industry to businesses and consumers as the main source of funding in Malaysia.

From Figure 2.3, we can see that the ratio of private credit to gross domestic product (GDP) grew steadily until 1986. From 1985 on, Malaysia experienced a massive crisis triggered by the high interest rate policy implemented by the US government in the 1980s. Commodity prices dropped dramatically and price reductions affected many developing countries that relied strongly on commodity exports. Commodity price volatility further affected the new Heavy Industries Corporation of Malaysia (HICOM). Due to the crisis, many corporations filed for bankruptcy, leading to a significant reduction in lending (Athukorala, 2010). This led in turn to a decrease in private credit from 98.22% of GDP in 1986 to 67.50% in 1991, as a result of the slowdown in business and closure of many corporations. It can also be noticed that the amount of deposits was also affected during the 1985 recession, with a reduction from 122.19% of GDP in 1986 to 52.87% in 1991 (Figure 2.3). Recovery began in 1992, and private credit reached 155.25% of GDP in 1998.

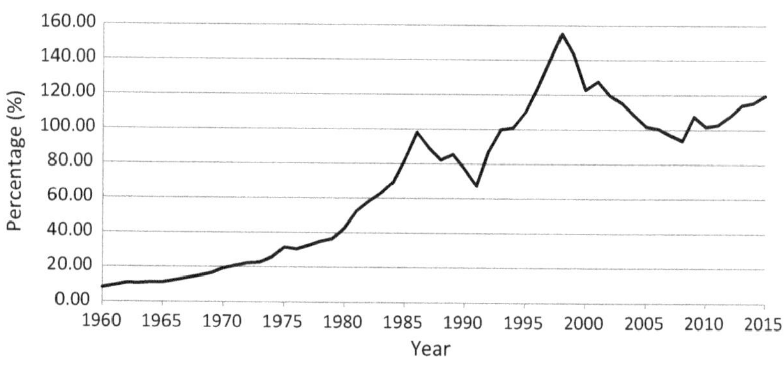

Figure 2.3 Private credit as percentage of GDP for domestic banks in Malaysia

Source: Financial Development and Structure Dataset, The World Bank (Beck et al., 2015)

The banking industry in Malaysia was again affected during the AFC or "Tomyam Goong" crisis of 1997. The most badly affected sector was private credit. Figure 2.3 shows the private credit as a percentage of GDP for the domestic banks in Malaysia from 1960 to 2015. This reached its peak of 155.25% during the AFC period because the crisis had caused industry to restrict lending activities and to further revise the criteria of the creditworthiness of lenders. This significantly affected the economy in Malaysia. BNM reduced the Statutory Reserve Requirement from 13.7% in February 1998 to 4% in September 1998 to facilitate lending activities in the economy (BNM Annual Report, 1998). Private credit slowly recovered and increased to 107.57% in 2009, despite the GFC. This shows that the Malaysian banking industry was less prone to the effects of GFC than developed economies. In the perspective of bank deposit as a percentage of GDP, the AFC may not have affected the Malaysian banks deposit position as bad as the private credit, where the reduction in the deposit rates were reduced from 8.51% in 1998 to 4.12% in 1999 and further fell to 3% in 2005 (Source: Thomson Datastream). However, the statistic showed that the domestic banks deposit as a percentage of GDP remained above 100% after 1996 to 2015 (refer to Figure 2.4).

Clearly the episodic economic crises in Malaysia greatly affected Malaysian banking activities and led to further slowdowns in economic activity. This is due to the low confidence from investors during the country's economic downturns. Various fiscal and monetary policies were therefore implemented in order to bring the economy back to the normal level for

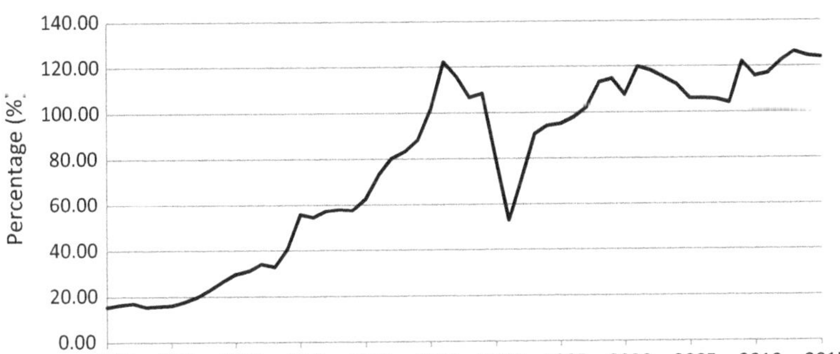

Figure 2.4 Bank deposits as a percentage of GDP for domestic banks in Malaysia

Source: Financial Development and Structure Dataset, The World Bank (Beck et al., 2015)

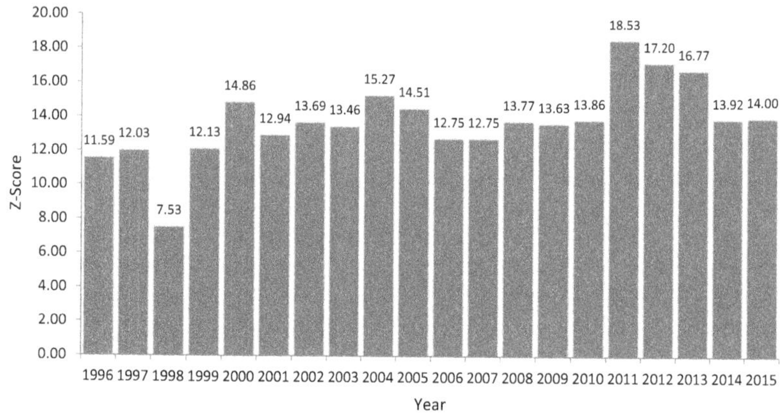

Figure 2.5 Bank Z-scores

Source: Financial Development and Structure Dataset, The World Bank (Beck et al., 2015)

long-term sustainability. Further, strengthening the banking industry was deemed to be important to the Malaysian economy, as the banking industry in Malaysia is the main channel for monetary policy transmission. This is because the banking industry is the main source of funding for businesses in the economy of a developing country such as Malaysia. The role of BNM as the central bank thus remains crucial in guaranteeing the smooth functioning of the economy by safeguarding the banking industry, creating a resilient and sound banking industry, and ensuring a better functioning payments and financial system in Malaysia.

The health of the banking industry in Malaysia is shown in Figure 2.5 as the bank solvency ratio in terms of the Z-score. The solvency of banks in Malaysia was greatly affected during the AFC, with the Z-score decreasing from 12.03 in 1997 to 7.53 in 1998.

After the year 2000, Malaysian banks were instructed by BNM to merge into ten anchor banks. This forced merger was considered successful and has translated into a stable bank solvency rate in the 2000s. As Figure 2.5 indicates, the Malaysian banks' solvency rates ranged from 12.75 to 15.27 from 2000 to 2006.The impressive solvency rates of the domestic banks show the success of the merger process in bringing the banks back from financial distress during the AFC. Solvency has grown steadily over the years since 2001, from 12.94 to 15.27 in 2004. In fact, banks did not suffer much from the GFC, as solvency continued to increase from 12.75 in 2007 to 13.63 in 2009. In 2011, following the AFC and GFC periods, the solvency rate was at its highest ever value of 18.53. The good solvency rates for these domestic banks signify that the fundamentals of the Malaysian banking industry remained strong, even as banks in developed countries were severely affected.

2.1.2 Financial liberalization

Malaysian financial markets have experienced stages of liberalization, due to the crisis periods in the 1980s and 1990s. The government implemented the forced merger exercise following the AFC period with the aim of strengthening these banks in response to the unexpected external turmoil in the post-AFC period. Apart from the forced merger strategy, the government also increased restrictions on opening new branches and installing new ATMs, for both domestic and foreign commercial banks. In Malaysia, foreign commercial banks are allowed to own a maximum of 30% of domestic commercial banks, or 49% of other financial firms (Yusoff, Hasan and Jalil, 2000).

The number of foreign banks increased from 13 in 1998 to 20 in 2016. Figure 2.6 presents the percentage of foreign banks among all banks in Malaysia: It increases steadily from 30% in 2003 to 42% in 2015, which marks the significant presence of foreign banks in Malaysia following the enactment of the Financial Services Acts (FSA) 2003. The FSA 2003 provides the basic infrastructure for foreign financial institutions to expand their business in Malaysia and to further contribute to efficiency and build a more

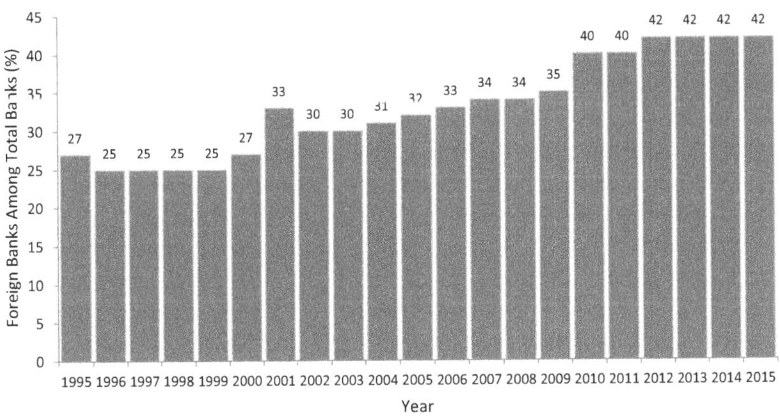

Figure 2.6 Foreign banks as a percentage of all banks

Source: Financial Development and Structure Dataset, The World Bank (Beck et al., 2015)

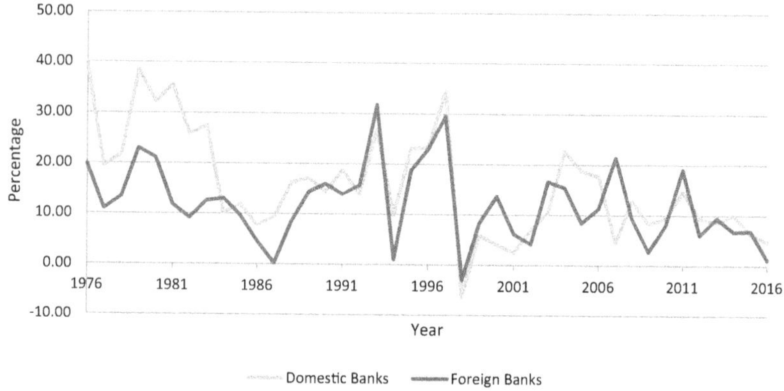

Figure 2.7 Growth of total assets of domestic and foreign banks, 1976–2016

Source: Financial Development and Structure Dataset, The World Bank (Beck et al., 2015)

developed banking and financial system (BNM Annual Report, 2003). This is crucial for the Malaysian economy, as it enables a more resilient, sound, and better developed financial system that can bring the country towards a fully developed economy.

The growth in total assets of foreign banks overtook the growth in total assets of domestic banks in Malaysia in 1998, as can be seen in Figure 2.7. Much of the academic literature supports having foreign banks competing in the local banking system. One of the benefits highlighted by Levine (1996) is that the presence of foreign banks will led to the adoption of more advanced technology by the domestic banks, to strengthen their presence and compete better with their foreign counterparts. Hence, the entrance of foreign banks into the Malaysia banking system is a vital milestone for the industry, creating a better technology spillover favouring the domestic banks and enhancing the overall banking industry in Malaysia.

Further reformation and liberalization policies were introduced under the Financial Sector Master Plan I (FSMP I: 2001–2010) after the AFC period, which aimed to continue to enhance the Malaysian banking system's resilience (BNM Annual Report, 2000). FSMP I focused on the post-AFC recovery measures that aim to improve the financial system in Malaysia by developing a more resilient and competitive financial system that contributes to economic growth in the long run. Besides, the FSMP I also aims to develop a dynamic financial system with stronger and forward-looking domestic financial institutions which are technologically driven. This is vital in facing the continuous challenges of globalization and liberalization.

In 2009, the Malaysian government introduced FSMP II for the years 2011–2020, with a similar objective. It continues to increase the overall financial stability and optimize the opportunities available to both domestic and foreign banks (BNM Annual Report, 2009). In order to benefit from the positive spillover from foreign banks' participation in the local market, the Financial Sector Blueprint further outlined the criteria for setting up foreign banks in Malaysia. Under the Financial Services Act, passed in late 2012 in conjunction with the Financial Sector Blueprint (2011–2020), the issuance of new licenses to foreign banks must serve the best interests of the Malaysian economy (BNM Annual Report, 2012). Based on the blueprint, the central bank has imposed prudential selection criteria toward any new foreign banks which are interested in operating in Malaysia. The selection criteria includes a stable financial and business record, established and well-experienced, high integrity values displayed by their foreign investor, and that have a potential business plan that is sound and feasible to carry out in Malaysia. The foreign bank selective prudential criteria were implemented with the aim of creating a better financial system in Malaysia by encouraging the establishment of foreign banks that are able to contribute positively to the advancement in financial products and services development, risk management expertise, and more transparent payment and financial systems.

FSMP II outlines a financial liberalization that encompasses the following:

i) Offering more new foreign licenses, including Islamic banking licenses, commercial banking licenses, and *takaful* licenses to share the expertise that is absent from the domestic financial market.
ii) Encourage domestic banks to seek potential strategic alliances with their foreign counterpart to increase their global presence; such alliances can help the Malaysian government to increase foreign equity limits by up to 70%.
iii) Promote more flexible operation policies for locally incorporated foreign commercial banks to open more branches in a smaller area.

This financial liberalization has increased the flexibility of foreign bank entry requirements into the domestic financial market. Domestic banks will benefit from their presence in the market. The government believes that these foreign banks will create healthy competition among the local banks. To maintain the competitiveness in the industry, these local banks will attempt to enhance the quality of their product and services, to diversify product innovations, and to engage in technologies serving their customers.

Similar to local banks, the intense surveillance and supervision by BNM's Financial Stability Board of these foreign banks is implemented to preserve Malaysian financial stability and to avoid unpredictable shocks being created by these banks' activities.

Apart from reducing the operating flexibility of foreign banks in Malaysia, FSMP II also outlined the accessibility of local banks, which can be accessed from most rural areas in Malaysia via agent banking. The agent banking concept was introduced in 2012, allowing domestic banks to provide other alternatives to customers seeking financial services in underserved and remote areas (BNM Annual Report, 2012). These agents serve the licensed financial institutions' customers via third-party outlets, such as stores, petrol stations, telecommunication agents, and post offices throughout Malaysia. The concept of agent banking has enhanced the accessibility of financial services, which can now be reached by customers for lower cost, even in remote areas.

Financial liberalization has been well-documented in the academic literature (for example, Girardone, Molyneux and Gardener, 2004; Stewart, Matousek and Nguyen, 2016) as improving the financial infrastructure of many countries. The post-AFC period created a different banking landscape for many national banking industries in the ASEAN region. After many measures were imposed to strengthen banking systems, the policy makers in ASEAN countries further implemented financial liberalization measures to cause their domestic banks to be competitive and able to absorb dynamic market changes. This again marks the importance of financial liberalization in enhancing the banking industry in both the ASEAN region and Malaysia. Nevertheless, a more integrated banking industry may expose the local banking industry to a high-risk spillover effect, due to domestic banks competing for deposits with foreign banks, further affecting the level of profitability and leading to moral hazards (Hellmann, Murdock and Stiglitz, 2000).

The wave of financial liberalization continued with the endorsement of the ASEAN Banking Integration Framework (ABIF) in December 2014 by the ASEAN Central Bank Governors. ABIF allows banks to penetrate into the ASEAN banking industry by permitting those banks with sufficiently strong fundamentals to gain greater access to ASEAN markets and more flexibility in their operations. This allows the Malaysian banks with strong fundamentals to further expand in ASEAN markets. This will create more integrated banking sectors, especially in the ASEAN region, undeniably leading to greater competition, improving the quality of banking and financial services in the region. Further, the ABIF is expected to spur trade and investment in ASEAN, because it helps small and medium enterprises (SMEs) to more easily access financing. It does so by increasing the lending capacity of ASEAN banks, and strong regional banks will utilize their advanced technology to reach out to wider market shares in the region.

In 2016, the latest development in the Malaysian banking sector is the promotion of technology advancements to serve the customers and international links of the local financial system. Technology adoption is more crucial for serving technology-savvy customers, compared to traditional financial service delivery channels. BNM reported a huge increase of 98.1% in mobile banking transactions, amounting to RM62.6 million, in 2016. To encourage more innovation in delivering services to customers, Malaysian banks are encouraged to collaborate with the proliferation of financial technology companies. Such collaboration is intended to tap into the enormous opportunity of technological advancement, such as biometric authentication methods for new banking customers, artificial intelligence (AI) for serving customers, and contactless payment. In 2016, there are 57 licensed financial institutions, consisting of 29 domestic banks and 28 foreign-owned banks.

The financial liberalization process and the introduction of the FSMP II further altered the banking landscape in Malaysia, with banking concentration reducing significantly from 92.74% in 2010 to 53.55% in 2011 – a total reduction of 39.19% (Figure 2.8). This reduction indicates that the banking industry is now less dominated by the big banks

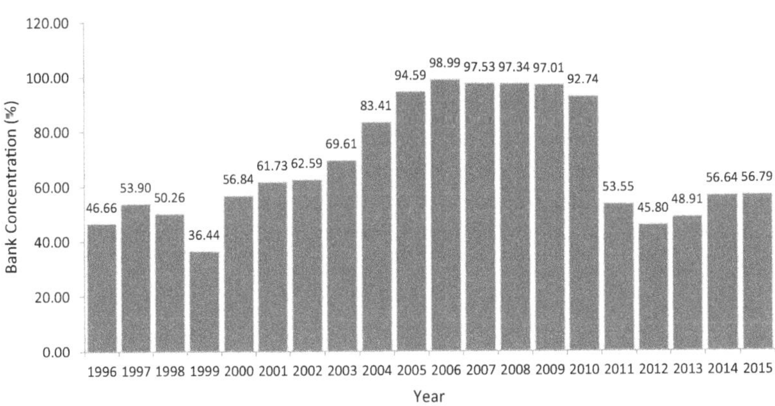

Figure 2.8 Bank concentration (percentage)

Source: Financial Development and Structure Dataset, The World Bank (Beck et al., 2015)

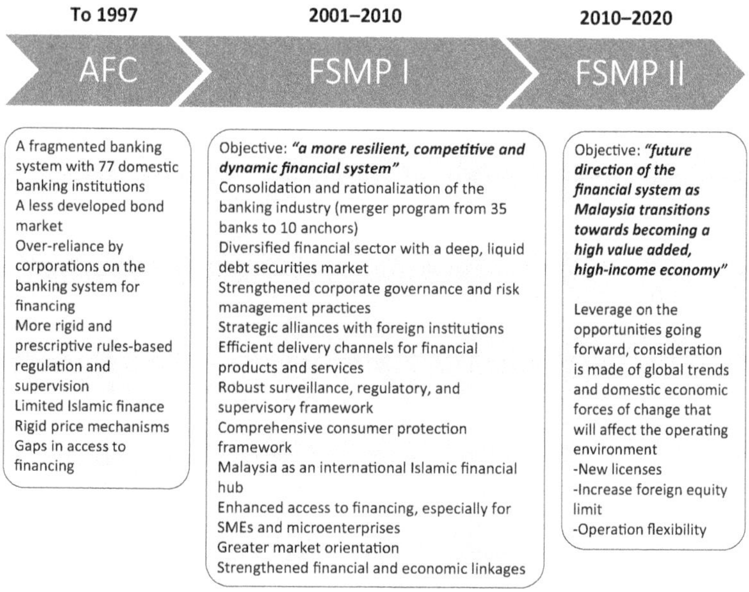

Figure 2.9 The evolution of the Malaysian banking landscape post-AFC

Sources: Financial Sector Master Plans I and II, BNM

than in previous years. This is because the forced merger that ended in December 2000 received criticism due to the increase in bank concentration, where a few banks dominated the markets, resulting in inefficiency in the industry on account of the decrease in competition. Reduction in bank concentration also makes the banking industry more competitive and hence the banks need to be more efficient for long-term sustainability (see Figure 2.9). This is because a more concentrated banking industry gave greater freedom for the banks to act and hence resulted in excessive risk-taking behaviour to earn higher returns (Uhde and Heimeshoff, 2009).

2.1.3 *Islamic banking*

Malaysia's 30-year-old Islamic finance industry puts the country among the best established Islamic financial hubs in the world. The enactment of the Islamic Banking Act 1983 enabled the establishment of the country's first Islamic Bank, Bank Islam Malaysia Berhad, in July 1983. Prior to 1998, the inception of Islamic banking was initiated through window-based banking, where existing conventional banks were allowed to offer "interest-free banking" products and services to their customers. The window-based banking scheme encouraged almost a majority of conventional Malaysian banks to offer Islamic banking products and services. Apart from serving the local Muslim customer by providing an Islamic financial services alternative alongside the conventional product and services, Islamic banking serves as an intermediate for mobilizing funds for production purposes (Abdul-Mahid, Saal and Battisti, 2010). The term "interest-free banking" was replaced by "Islamic banking" in 1998. In 1999, the second Islamic bank was established in Malaysia (Bank Muamalat) (BNM Annual Report, 1999).

The total assets of Islamic banks in Malaysia for the period 2001 to 2016 are presented in Table 2.1. Prior to 2000, the Islamic banking sector followed an outstanding upward trend, registering an average 49% total asset

Table 2.1 Total assets for Malaysian Islamic banks

Year	*Islamic banks Total asset (millions)*	*Growth rate*
2001	58.929	
2002	68.07	15.5%
2003	82.196	20.8%
2004	94.6	15.1%
2005	111.8	18.2%
2006	133	19.0%
2007	152.93	15.0%
2008	188.10	23.0%
2009	228.55	21.5%
2010	262.38	14.8%
2011	328.65	25.3%
2012	375.95	14.4%
2013	426.64	13.5%
2014	477.06	11.8%
2015	535.35	12.2%
2016	563.23	5.2%
Average growth rate sub period 1: 2002–2006		***17.7%***
Average growth rate sub period 2: 2007–2011		***20.0%***
Average growth rate sub period 3: 2012–2016		***11.4%***

Source: Islamic banking system: Statement of assets from various issues of the monthly statistical bulletin of Malaysia and Bank Negara Malaysia

annual growth over the period 1995–1999. This upward trend in performance continued in 2000. According to BNM, the sector continued to display an outstanding asset growth of 30%, reaching RM47.1 billion in 2000. The total deposits and financing of the sector increased to RM35.9 billion and RM20.9 billion, respectively. Maintaining the same strong momentum, the average growth rate of total assets for Malaysian Islamic banks for the sub periods 2002–2006, 2007–2011, and 2012–2016 were 17.7%, 20%, and 11.4%, respectively. During the first sub period, various measures and strategies were proposed as part of FSMP I to enhance the total assets growth rate of 20% for Islamic banks as a percentage of Malaysian banking total asset.

FSMP I had three effects on the Islamic banking sector: i) increasing the sector's institutional capacity by creating more professionals in the Islamic finance sector who are competent in technical finance and Shariah understanding; ii) financial infrastructure development by promoting Islamic product innovation among Islamic financial institutions and risk management instruments; and iii) regulatory framework development by creating a clear and distinct platform for Islamic as against conventional banking. In 2001, BNM imposed two measures on the Islamic banking sector: i) to disclose their capital adequacy ratio separately for their Islamic portfolio (a minimum of 8% for their weighted capital ratio); and ii) to standardize the calculation of the rate of return across all Islamic banking scheme banks. Apart from that, Islamic Banking and Finance Institute Malaysia (IBFIM) was established in 2002 as an institution responsible for producing more Islamic banking professionals to serve the Islamic banking sector (BNM Annual Report, 2002). Due to the aggressive measures taken by the regulators and Islamic banks during the first sub period, the targeted 20% growth rate was achieved in 2003, where a growth rate of 20.8% was reported, compared to 2002.

During 2003, the Malaysian Islamic banking sector consisted of 33 Islamic banking institutions (IBS) and 31 conventional banking institutions offering Islamic banking products and services (BNM Annual Report, 2003). Applying the concept of *bai' bithaman ajil* (BBA), BNM introduced an Islamic variable rate mechanism in the same year. This variable rate mechanism allows Islamic banking institutions to offer their customers a more competitive rate than a fixed rate (BNM Annual Report, 2004). The first sub period also saw a liberalization of the Islamic banking sector, with three full-fledged foreign banks being given the license to serve as Islamic financial institutions in Malaysia – namely, Kuwait Finance House, Al-Rajhi Banking and Investment Bank, and a consortium of Islamic institutions from Qatar (Qatar Islamic Bank, Global Investment Bank, and RUSD Investment Bank). The presence of these banks helps increase the quality of products and services provided by the local institutions, in order to stay competitive in the Islamic banking industry. These fully fledged foreign banks are believed to provide more innovative Islamic products and services, ranging from retail, investment, wealth and fund management, real estate development, and venture capital business.

An average 20% total asset growth rate was achieved during the second sub period (2006–2011). To support the liberalization of the Islamic banking sector, the central bank has further loosened up the operational flexibility requirement of Islamic foreign banks in 2010, allowing these foreign banks to open more new branches to serve local customers better. There is a wider range of Islamic products and services (over 100), ranging from simple *al wadiah* deposit products to Islamic structured investment products (BNM Annual Report, 2010). The greatest total asset growth rate for the Islamic banking sector was recorded as 25% in 2011 – among the highest growth rates in decades. The Malaysian Islamic Financial sector has continued to roll out FSMP II (2011–2020), where further measures and strategies are introduced to strengthen the presence of the Islamic banking sector alongside of the conventional banking sector in Malaysia. FSMP II aims to strengthen the financial system in Malaysia to become a developed nation with a high value-added and high income economy.

The presence of local Islamic financial institutions on a global platform promotes the diversity of market players that can provide quality financial products and services to the public and further enhance market efficiency via standard product documentation and agreement, as well as increased international linkage activities via strategic alliances with other financial institutions in other countries. A slower but still double-digit growth rate (11.4%) was registered during the third sub period (2012–2016). Currently, according to Bank Negara Malaysia, there are **ten** fully fledged Islamic banks and **six** foreign-owned entities in Malaysia (see Table 2.2). With the strong demand from Muslim and non-Muslim customers, the Malaysian Islamic banking industry's assets have recorded a steady double-digit growth over the decades. As of 2016, the top **five** conventional and Islamic

Table 2.2 List of Islamic financial institutions in Malaysia

Domestic Islamic institutions	*Foreign Islamic institutions*
Affin Islamic Bank Berhad	Al-Rajhi Banking and Investment Corporation (Malaysia) Berhad
AmBank Islamic Berhad	Asian Finance Bank Berhad
Bank Islam Malaysia Berhad	HSBC Amanah Malaysia Berhad
Bank Muamalat Malaysia Berhad	Kuwait Finance House (Malaysia) Berhad
CIMB Islamic Bank Berhad	OCBC Al-Amin Bank Berhad
Hong Leong Islamic Bank Berhad	Standard Chartered Saadiq Berhad
Maybank Islamic Berhad	
OCBC Al-Amin Bank Berhad	
Public Islamic Bank Berhad	
RHB Islamic Bank Berhad	

Source: BNM Annual Report (2017)

Conventional Banks

Bank	Total Assets	Year of Establishment	Ownership Type	Number of Branches
MALAYAN BANKING BERHAD	RM 496.063 billion	1960	Local	2400
PUBLIC BANK BERHAD	RM 380.053 billion	1966	Local	389
CIMB BERHAD	RM 376.306 billion	1974	Local	909
RHB BERHAD	RM 236.679 billion	1997	Local	332 conventional and Islamic
HONG LEONG BANK BERHAD	RM 210.475 billion	1968	Local	300 local and global

Islamic Banks

Bank	Total Assets	Year of Establishment	Ownership Type	Number of Branches
MAYBANK ISLAMIC	RM 181.794 billion	2008	Local	14 dedicated branches and co-located at more than 400 Maybank branches
BANK ISLAM MALAYSIA BERHAD	RM 55.677 billion	1983	Local	145
PUBLIC ISLAMIC BERHAD	RM 49.663 billion	2008	Local	256
BANK MUAMALAT MALAYSIA BERHAD	RM 22.637 billion	1999	Local	61
CIMB ISLAMIC BERHAD	RM 11.228 billion	2003	Local	collocated with CIMB bank branches

Figure 2.10 Total assets for conventional banks versus Islamic banks in Malaysia (as of 2016)

banks in term of asset value are presented in Figure 2.10. Rating agency Malaysia projected the growth to increase to 25% by the year 2017. The average growth rate of Islamic banking assets is expected to be 13% annually and to further grow to US$296.29 billion by the year 2019.

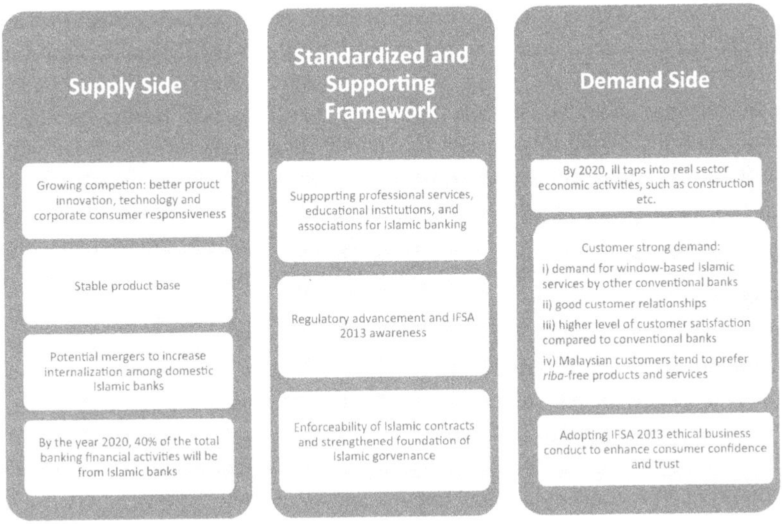

Figure 2.11 Determinants of sustainable growth in Malaysian Islamic banks

Source: Malaysia Islamic Financial Report 2015 (p. 115)

Overall, total assets have been growing at a steady rate of between 5.2% and 25.3% per year. In fact, the growth in total assets continues even during the GFC period, and this indicates that the Islamic banks in the country were strong enough to survive the financial crisis. Based on Figure 2.11, the strong growth rate displayed by Islamic banking total assets can be attributed to three factors: strong performance on the supply side (Islamic banking service providers), a highly regulated and supporting framework, and a promising demand for Islamic products and services from Malaysian customers (Malaysian Islamic Financial Report, 2015).

From the supply side, the tremendous growth in the assets of the Islamic banking sector is due to the increase in the quality of Islamic products and services by domestic Islamic banks. The financial liberalization in this sector has allowed many foreign banks to operate in Malaysia; these have introduced many innovative Islamic products to the market. Their presence in the market has directly caused the domestic Islamic banking market to become more competitive. The domestic Islamic banks are more innovative in introducing many new products and services to their customers in order to sustain their presence in this intense Islamic banking market. In addition, an investment account platform (a multi-bank platform) was introduced by BNM in 2016 to channel the individual, corporate, and institutional funds that are available in four big Islamic banks so as to finance common investment options and many innovative SME projects (Islamic Financial Services Industry Stability Report, 2016). This will further enhance the capability of the local banks to channel their funds towards financing more potential growth projects.

Apart from this, the Islamic Financial Services Act (2013) clearly distinguished deposit and investment accounts. With this new requirement, the Mudharabah account previously known as the deposit account was reclassified as an investment account. Changes of this sort will be further required if Islamic banks are to become more transparent in distinguishing their account types. This is crucial for customers: The new requirement allows them to gauge the risk associated with each type of account. Further, the possibility of a merger exercise among Islamic banks is very welcomed by BNM, as it would create a stronger Islamic bank prepared to engage in wholesale banking services and even to spread abroad.

The second determinant of the outstanding growth rate was the contribution of the strong foundation and regulatory framework outline by BNM. BNM played a significant role in revising the framework to ensure suitable supervisory enforcement is introduced to maintain the sustainability of Islamic bank functions in this challengingly instable market. The IFSA 2013 outlines the comprehensive legal framework for the development of Islamic finance in Malaysia. This includes a comprehensive and detailed regulatory framework on various Islamic financial contracts and supports on the effective and efficient implementation on Shariah contracts to offer Islamic financial products and services. In addition, BNM ensures that the four-contract framework of Shariah standards, operational standards, oversight function, and resolution are all strictly followed by Islamic banks. The role of the new institutions is to continue to produce quality Islamic banking professionals.

Finally, from the demand side, the asset growth rate contributes through strong demand from the real economy, and from retail/corporate/institutional customer demand. As for the real sector, Islamic banks have the opportunity to finance larger government projects, such as federal infrastructure construction projects, etc. From the perspective of customers, Islamic banks can increase their customer base by providing quality services, a higher level of customer satisfaction than with conventional bank customers, good long-term customer relationships, and a level of awareness of non-*riba* banking transaction among Islamic customer; in this way, they have increased the participation of non-Muslim customers that opt for more transparent and ethical banking services.

2.2 Bank efficiency

The performance of depository institutions has been a focus of attention by many researchers. The sustainability of these institutions is one of the main determinants of economic prosperity (Zhang and Daly, 2014). Poor performance leads to major financial disruptions for a country and further pressures the country's economic growth rate (El-Gamal and Inanoglu, 2005). Hence, early researchers have explored various measures that enable bank performance to be captured via bank efficiency. The study of bank efficiency dates back to the early 1990s, especially in the European and developed countries, and includes, e.g., Aly et al. (1990); Ferrier and Lovell (1990); McAllister and McManus (1993); Elyasiani et al. (1994); Berg et al. (1993); Favero and Papi (1993); and Wheelock and Wilson (1995). The empirical evidence to date has explored different types of bank efficiency including cost efficiency, profit efficiency (for example Poshakwale and Qian, 2011; Řepková, 2015; Stewart, Matousek and Nguyen, 2016), and technical efficiency (Guzman and Reverte, 2008; Das and Kumbhakar, 2012; Stewart, Matousek and Nguyen, 2016).

2.2.1 Bank efficiency during crisis periods

Economic turbulences have been said to occur in cycles, perhaps with a crisis every decade (Schularick and Taylor, 2012). Crises lead to disruption of the financial system and affect the country's economic health, either regionally or globally. During the crisis, researchers found that banking operations were badly affected, leading to profit, cost, and technical inefficiencies. Due to the excessive currency speculation in Thailand in the 1990s, the currency devaluation effect spilled through the other ASEAN regions, and ASEAN banks returned their worst performance in history. Various measures were implemented by the government as recovery programs for the banks. However, due to different levels of technological, regulatory, and environmental conditions across the different ASEAN countries, bank efficiency and speed of recovery from the AFC was found to be different. For example, Karim (2001) investigated the cost efficiency of the commercial banks in Malaysia, Thailand, the Philippines, and Indonesia for the period 1989 to 1996. The findings suggest that state-owned banks were more cost inefficient than the private banks in the ASEAN countries. He also found that the economies of scale of ASEAN banks reduce with size of the banks, with even larger banks exhibiting higher cost efficiency levels. He emphasized that Malaysian banks tended to be more scale-efficient and cost-efficient than Indonesia, Thailand, and Philippine banks. Malaysian banks were found to recover faster than the other three ASEAN banks. These inefficiencies may be due to restrictive regulatory banking systems that translated into higher inefficiency among banks, especially in Indonesia and the Philippines. Malaysian and Singapore maintained the best level of managerial and profitability efficiency among ASEAN members after the GFC period in 2008 (Wu et al., 2016). Sun and Chang (2011) found that most of the emerging Asian banks improved their cost efficiency after the AFC and that the GFC had a minor effect on them. Due to bank industry reformation within these Asian regions, most Asian countries have rebounded their level of bank efficiency, with Taiwan and Indonesia as exceptions. This emphasizes the importance of investigating each country's factors that determine their bank performance, as each country has its own unique banking and economic setting that makes bank performance different. However, the GFC had different results for Australian banks, with a negative effect on Australian bank's profit efficiency, but not on cost efficiency (Vu and Turnell, 2010).This cost inefficiency is possibly due to Australian banks tending to depend on deposits, and the cost to raise funds has become more expensive during the GFC period (Battellino, 2010).

In the context of the cost and technical frontier, Chen (2004) and Hu, Li and Chiu (2004) found that Taiwanese banks tended to perform lower in their technical efficiency aspect after the AFC period. A similar pattern was found by Gardener, Molyneux and Nguyen-Linh (2011), whose findings support the claim that Malaysian banks outperformed Indonesian and Thai banks in terms of their level of technical and cost efficiency after the AFC period. Consistent with Gardener, Molyneux and Nguyen-Linh (2011), Sufian (2010) analyzed the impact of the AFC on bank efficiency in Malaysia and Thailand from 1992 to 2003. The results suggest that the source of inefficiency is due to scale efficiency instead of pure technical efficiency, for both the Thai and Malaysian banking industries. The technical efficiency of the Malaysian banks improved after the Asian financial crisis, unlike the efficiency of Thai banks. Using a Bayesian dynamics approach, Tsionas, Assaf and Matousek (2015) investigated the technical and allocative efficiencies during and after the GFC within European Union banks. Their results show that European banks experienced a reduction in technical and allocative efficiencies after the GFC and improved performance over the long run. This supports the study by Erdem and Erdem (2008) which found that the GFC affected technical efficiency among Turkish banks.

2.2.2 *Bank efficiency and financial liberalization*

Many empirical studies have documented that financial liberalization and privatization can improve local bank performances. The common policy implemented during financial liberalization revised the foreign ownership policy, with the central government scaling back the restriction and making it more flexible for foreign banks' penetration in the domestic market. This flexibility will encourage more foreign banks to open operations in the domestic financial market. The influx of these foreign banks affected the performance of domestic banks both positively and negatively. Regarding profitability, Sturm and William (2004) suggest that these foreign banks do not necessary outperform the domestic banks. Similarly, banks with majority foreign ownership tend to underperform Latin American local banks in profit and cost efficiency (Figueira, Nellis and Parker, 2009). Additionally, a flexible foreign ownership policy worked to improve the overall efficiency of Turkish banks (El-Gamal and Inanoglu, 2005). Financial liberalization need not be implemented only within a country; it may also involve the formation of a single market for many countries. A single market such as the European Union (EU) has pros and cons regarding bank efficiency. The advantages of having a single market include promoting globalization of financial and technology innovations and deregulation (Stewart, Matousek and Nguyen, 2016) within countries, further minimizing cost (Hermes and Meesters, 2015). Apart from this, borderless banking activities can allow the market to experience a more intense competitive environment (Girardone, Molyneux and Gardener, 2004; Hermes and Meesters, 2015; Stewart, Matousek and Nguyen, 2016) and further dampen banks' profitability (Wu et al., 2016).

Hermes and Nhung (2010) identified the impact of financial liberalization on Latin American and Asian banks' technical efficiency. They found that the overall technical efficiency in Latin America and Asia was mainly from pure technical efficiency – that is, managerial practices. Besides, they found that financial liberalization improves the overall technical efficiency, pure technical efficiency, and scale efficiency. In the context of the Asian region, Burki and Niazi (2010) found that foreign banks performed better in terms of technical efficiency than public and private banks in Pakistan, in their analysis of financial reform in Pakistan from 1991 to 2000. They explain that the higher efficiency level of the foreign banks is because of their superior banking and customer support services. Further, they found that foreign banks outperformed the public and private banks in terms of cost efficiency before the financial reform and the first-reform period (1993–1996). However, the cost efficiency of foreign banks compared to the private banks fell around 1998, due to the freezing of foreign currency accounts, which resulted in a dramatic fall in foreign currency deposits at foreign banks and also a shrinkage in their assets. Besides, public banks also exhibited a lower allocative efficiency level than the private and foreign banks, due to managers' inability to choose the right mix of inputs, an inability arising from their lack of independence from the government. In the same view, Ataullah,

Cockerill and Le (2004) found that state-owned banks suffer from worse pure technical efficiency levels. They suggest that these state-owned banks need to downsize their operating scale in the long run in order to improve their return to scale.

In Taiwan, in the analysis of risk-adjusted efficiency of 26 Taiwanese banks, Chang and Chiu (2006) found that the root cause of cost inefficiency of the banks is from technical efficiency. They indicated that the banks' inefficiency is mainly due to underutilization of inputs. This is consistent with the results of Chen (2004), who also found that technical inefficiency was the cause of cost inefficiency for Taiwanese banks from 1994 to 2000. Furthermore, he also found that the source of technical efficiency comes mainly from scale efficiency, rather than from pure technical efficiency. Hence, similar to India, the banks suffer from pure worse technical efficiency due to their underutilization of inputs.

Matthews and Ismail (2006) investigated the efficiency and productivity growth of the domestic and foreign commercial banks in Malaysia for the period between 1994 and 2000. Similar to the Pakistani banks, the foreign banks in Malaysia experience higher technical efficiency than the domestic banks. They also found that the scale inefficiency was the main cause of inefficiency in the Malaysian banking industry. Similarly, Sufian (2009) also found that scale inefficiency is the major problem for the Malaysian banking industry in his analysis of the determinants of bank efficiency during the AFC from 1995 to 1999. He also found that foreign banks are relatively technically efficient, compared to domestic banks in Malaysia.

Since the financial reformation, privatization has been another strategy implemented by regulators to strengthen local bank performance to face intense competition with these foreign banks in the market. El-Gamal and Inanoglu (2005) and Kraft, Hofler and Payne (2006) found that privatization does not immediately affect a bank's cost efficiency. Kraft, Hofler and Payne (2006) suggest that cost efficiency derives from better overall management teams and effective risk management strategies, as implemented by Croatian banks. The Chinese government introduced an open market policy in the 1990s by joining the World Trade Organization, and smaller local banks were unable to compete with the foreign banks introduced during that time. The findings of Yao et al. (2007) show that those Chinese local banks that were small or had less access to economies of scale failed to cope with the foreign banks' level of efficiency. Yao et al. (2007) highlight that competition with foreign banks is the greatest challenge for the local Chinese banks. A radical reformation needs to be implemented, and the focus of the reformation should be related not only to recapitalization, but should also focus on enhancing the competence of the local banks' management teams to deal with a more competitive environment.

Gilbert and Wilson (1998) describe that the bank reformation of 1991 improved the technical efficiency of Korean banks. The findings of Williams and Nguyen (2005) support the improvement in technical efficiency at Korean, Malaysian, Thailand, and Philippine banks after the financial liberalization. Ataullah, Cockerill and Le (2004) investigate the effect of financial liberalization on bank efficiency in India and Pakistan between years 1988 and 1998. Results suggest that overall technical efficiency of the Indian banking industry improved from 67.9% before liberalization to 79.9% after it. The increase in the overall efficiency level is due to both pure technical efficiency and scale efficiency. On the other hand, in Pakistan, the overall technical efficiency improved from 38.6% to 47.8% after the liberalization process. The improvement in the efficiency of the Pakistan banking industry was mainly due to scale efficiency, with the government allowing the public sector banks to reduce the number of employees and close unprofitable branches in rural areas. Nevertheless, the Pakistan banking industry still suffers from low pure technical efficiency, even after financial liberalization which mainly affected the state-owned banks. This is because of the high political instability that challenged the commitment by government in the liberalization process. This is shown by relatively low technical efficiency scores of the state-owned banks, as compared to those of foreign banks in Pakistan. Nevertheless, the state-owned banks performed better than their private and foreign counterparts throughout the sample period. This is consistent with the earliest study of bank efficiency in India by Bhattacharya et al. (1997) during the pre-financial liberalization period. The study is also consistent with the earlier studies of Mohan and Ray (2004); Das et al. (2005); and Sensarma (2005). Das and Kumbhakar (2012) further examined the impact of deregulation on the banking industry in India from 1996 to 2005. Similar to Ataullah, Cockerill and Le (2004), they found that state-owned banks are relatively more technically efficient than the private and foreign banks, mainly on account of improvements in capital adequacy ratio. They suggest that private and foreign banks could further improve their scale efficiency by downsizing their operations, because these banks are operating far above their efficiency scale.

2.2.3 Bank efficiency and mergers/bank consolidation

Merger and acquisition are of major interest to banking authorities, policy makers, and researchers. Many governments promote bank consolidation and merger exercises as a financial liberalization reformation policy that can strengthen the presence of their domestic banks during the influx of foreign banks into their domestic bank industry. The merger exercise can be within local banks (Kasman and Yildirim, 2006; Jonas and King, 2008) or between foreign and local banks (Poghosyan and Poghosyan, 2010). Empirically, foreign bank entry has been found to increase the level of competition in the domestic banking industry and to further improve the level of local bank efficiency (Lehner and Schnitzer, 2008). However, this improvement tends to vary between emerging and more developed markets (Claessens, Demirgüç-Kunt and Huizinga, 2001). Many researchers have investigated the effects of merger exercises on bank performance in the most developed markets (Mishkin and Strahan, 1999; Poghosyan and Poghosyan, 2010; Fang, Hasan and Marton, 2011). From the point of view of cost efficiency, Poghosyan and Poghosyan (2010) found that foreign greenfield banks tended to outperform local or foreign-acquirer banks. The findings suggest that foreign-acquirer banks do not benefit from mergers with local banks. This may be due to the inefficiency of management teams following the merger exercise. In contrast, Jonas and King (2008) support the effectiveness of bank consolidation among US banks, where cost efficiency could be achieved when banks tended to adopt more advanced information technology to provide their services to customers and remain competitive. The advanced technologies adopted by banks following bank consolidation and merger exercises led to reductions in transaction costs and informational asymmetries associated with lending (Mishkin and Strahan, 1999). Fang, Hasan and Marton (2011) assert that foreign-acquirer banks are likely to enjoy better profit efficiency but lower cost efficiency than local banks in southeastern Europe. Generally many researchers have suggested that foreign-acquirers performed better than the domestic banks because of their advantages in terms of management team, lower cost of funds, technological advantages, and lower legal costs (see Kasman and Yildirim, 2006). Unlike in the case of developed markets, the empirical evidence regarding the effects of mergers on banks' efficiency in emerging countries is very much under explored.

As with the profit and cost efficiency findings, the literature indicates that the advantages of the bank consolidation and merger exercises translate into better technical and cost efficiency among domestic banks in the US (Kohers, Huang and Kohers, 2000; Al-Sharkas, Hassan and Lawrence, 2008) and in Lebanon (Turk Ariss, 2008). In the aftermath of the AFC, many regulators in the emerging market understood the significance of having strong and stable financial systems capable of absorbing unpredictable shocks. Similar to the merger and acquisition measures implemented in developed countries, the governments in the Asian region promoted bank consolidation and merger exercises as one measure to strengthen their domestic banks. A significant number of studies have explored the post-merger effects on cost and technical efficiency within Asian commercial banks. Within the Asian context, Kaur and Kaur (2010) explored the implication of mergers on the cost efficiency of Indian banks. They suggested that the average cost efficiency score of Indian public sector banks was 73.4%, while the value for private sector banks was 76.3%; the extension merger program implemented by the regulator was thus successful in the Indian banking sector. However, the merger between strong and distressed banks will not create a better synergy, since depositors will have no interest in depositing their savings in such distressed banks, ultimately reducing the asset quality of the stronger banks. Improvement in cost efficiency among Taiwanese banks was also found in Peng and Wang (2004). Some suggest that domestic banks do not benefit from merger and consolidation exercises (Srinivasan and Wall, 1992; Focarelli, Panetta and Salleo, 2002). The potential justifications for bank inefficiency were due to post-merger inefficient management teams and the broad agency cost problem between managers and shareholders (Piloff and Santomero, 1998).

Mergers among big banks are additionally found to pressure overall scale efficiency, as the efficiency gap between large and smaller banks becomes wider due to these smaller banks being unable to compete with the large banks in providing financial services to the market (Paul and Kourouche, 2008). After the mergers, the banking industry became more concentrated and the large banks received more market power, but ultimately reduced the overall bank efficiency. The Pakistan government implemented a bank consolidation strategy to strengthen local banks, since financial liberalization allowed foreign banks to freely compete with them. Burki and Niazi (2010) highlight that liberalization and intense competition pushed local Pakistani banks to enhance their level of technological innovation in serving their customers. In addition, the bank consolidation strategy translated into better technical efficiency performance for the local Pakistan banks than for the foreign banks.

Similar to Burki and Niazi (2010), Sufian and Habibullah (2009) and Krishnasamy et al. (2004) analyzed the effects of mergers and acquisitions among Malaysian banks during and after the AFC. Krishnasamy et al. (2004) examined the technical efficiency performance after the merger exercise and found that most of the affected banks had benefitted from the merger exercise. They infer that these affected banks showed an improvement in terms of technology and technical change. Consistent evidence was exhibited by Sufian and Habibullah (2009); however, the technical efficiency improvements among these Malaysian banks after the major banking consolidation was mainly due to the improvement in scale efficiency. Their results suggest that the consolidation resulted in more managerial efficiency in the banking industry, due to the expansion in the size of operations following banking consolidation. When Thoraneenitiyan and Avkiran (2009) tested cost and technical efficiency among the ASEAN countries collectively, they found that the merger process squeezed the level of efficiency scores. This might be due to external pressure, such as country-specific determinants and restructuring measures.

2.2.4 *Efficiency of Islamic banks versus conventional banks*

The concept of Islamic finance offers customers financial services that follow Islamic principles. Since the 2000s, the Malaysian banking sector has shown tremendous performance and has consistently registered a double-digit year-to-year growth rate. Due to this huge growth rate, researchers have focused on investigating how the performance of these Islamic banks compares to conventional banks. Empirical evidence supports the claim that the Islamic banks displayed lower cost efficiency than the conventional banks in Gulf Cooperation Council (GCC) countries (Alshammari, 2003) and Turkey (Alpay and Hassan, 2007). Contrary results were found by El-Gamal and Inanoglu (2005), suggesting that Turkish Islamic banks have better cost efficiency than their counterparts. They highlight that the existence of Islamic banks may not draw the conventional bank's customers away, and their presence tends to enhance the overall Turkish bank cost efficiency. Similar evidence was reported for Malaysian Islamic banks (Abdul-Majid, Md. Nor, and Said, 2005). In terms of profit efficiency, Samad (2004) found that Islamic banks performed as efficiently as conventional banks, though not for cost efficiency (Iqbal, 2001; Hassan, 2005). Rahim (2015) and Sufian and Kamarudin (2015) infer that domestic Islamic banks are found to be more cost-efficient, revenue-efficient, and profit-efficient than the foreign Islamic banks. The inefficiency among these foreign Islamic banks may be due to operation restrictions imposed by central banks that force them to open more branches and serve a larger customer base. In addition, Rahim (2015) suggest that domestic Islamic banks have the advantage of leverage on their conventional banks. Contrary results were reported for six GCC countries (Srairi, 2010), where the conventional banks in the tested GCC countries were found to be more profit-efficient and cost-efficient than their Islamic banks. The low profit efficiency for Islamic banks is likely due to their lower revenue efficiency (Srairi, 2010), which perhaps in turn is due to their customers being predisposed to Islamic products, regardless of the cost (Olson and Zoubi, 2008).

Regarding the technical efficiency frontier, Islamic banks were found to be relatively better than conventional banks for the period 1990–2000 among Turkish banks (Alpay and Hassan, 2007) and GCC banks (Al-Muharrami, 2008). Contrary evidence was also reported for the GCC countries (Mobarek and Kalonov, 2014; Johnes et al., 2014), Indonesian banks (Havidz and Setiawan, 2015), MENA and Asian banks (Rahman and Rosman, 2013), and Malaysian banks (Sufian, 2007; Rahim, 2015), where it was found that Islamic banks tend to be less efficient than conventional banks. The lower technical efficiency commonly found among Islamic banks may be due to three factors: i) the long process flow for introducing new Islamic banks' products and services, which must comply with

Shariah rules, and which thus incur high operational costs (Chapra, 2003), ii) the smaller size of Islamic banks compared to conventional banks tends to affect the technical efficiency level (Miller and Noulas, 1996; Drake et al., 2006), and iii) the domestically owed Islamic banks have been found to be less technically efficient than foreign-owned banks (Matthews and Ismail, 2006). In contrast with Mobarek and Kalonov (2014), Bader et al. (2008), Hassan et al. (2009), and Mokhtar et al. (2006) support the claim that the technical efficiency of Islamic banks in many tested countries is similar to that of conventional banks. On the other hand, Sufian (2007), Havidz and Setiawan (2015), and Yildirim (2015) suggest that Islamic banks' technical inefficiencies are more attributable to scale inefficiency rather than pure technical efficiency. They highlight the possibility that these banks operate on an inappropriate scale.

Consistent with Rahim (2015) and Sufian and Kamarudin (2015), Kamarudin et al. (2008) assert that domestic Islamic banks tend to outperform foreign Islamic banks. However, Mokhtar et al. (2008) reported that the foreign banks that offer Islamic windows are more technically efficient than the domestic Islamic windows. Their findings also support the claim that the overall technical efficiency of conventional banks outperforms that of Islamic banks in Malaysia.

Coinciding with the evidence for conventional banks, a long-lasting inverse effect on Islamic banks' level of technical efficiency is found after the AFC period (Abdul-Majid, Saal and Battisti, 2010). However, Willison (2009) and Yilmaz (2009) suggest that the Islamic banks' performance was not affected by the GFC. This is due to the highly regulated nature of the Islamic bank industry, which must ensure that investments are Shariah compliant and which are less likely to involve speculative and high-risk investments. Unlike the literature on conventional banks, it was also found that Islamic banks do not benefit from mergers and bank consolidation exercises, because bank management was disrupted by the merger process, the overall bank performances.

2.3 Malaysian bank efficiency

2.3.1 Data and methodology

The analysis of efficiency is based on the production frontier associated with the ability of banks to attain the maximum level of output given a level of inputs, or to minimize the level of input to production, given the output level. This definition has been used in technical efficiency analysis and is known as output orientation, while the latter is known as input orientation. On the other hand, cost efficiency is based on a cost frontier, which is defined as the ability of the management to minimize the cost function given a set of output and input prices. The profit efficiency is then defined as the ability of management to maximize the profits given a set of output and input prices.

The efficiency level is estimated based on the distance of each of the Decision Making Units (DMUs) – in our case, the individual banks – to the frontier. This can be calculated via parametric approaches or nonparametric approaches. One well-known parametric method to estimate the efficiency frontier is known as Stochastic Frontier Analysis (SFA), which is based on the Cobb–Douglas specification function. The major drawback of the parametric approach is that it imposes a particular function form being estimated and the distribution of efficiency. This can be solved using data envelopment analysis (DEA).

DEA is a nonparametric approach that uses linear programming techniques to compute the production frontier. Among its advantages are that DEA works well with small samples and requires no priori specification of the distribution of inefficiency or of a particular functional form. Nevertheless, the major drawback of DEA is that it assumes data to be free from measure error (Pasiouras, 2008). DEA comes out with the best-practice production frontier from a sample of DMUs through a piecewise linear programming. It derives from the combination of an actual input–output correspondence set that envelops the input–output correspondence of all DMUs in the sample study (Thanassoulis, 2001). Each DMU is then assigned an efficiency score that ranges between 0 and 1, with a score of 1 representing the most efficient DMU in the sample. DEA was first implemented with the assumption of constant return to scale (CRS), as proposed by Charnes, Cooper and Rhodes (1978). This model gives the overall technical efficiency scores with the assumption of a proportionate increase in both inputs and outputs. This was then modified by Banker, Charnes and Cooper (1984) to accommodate the disproportionate increase in inputs and outputs, giving a better representation of the efficiency level of the banks. The specification of DEA based on VRS is shown in Equation (1).

$$\begin{aligned} & \min_{\theta,\lambda} \theta, \\ & s.t. - y_q + Y\lambda \geq 0, \\ & \quad \theta x_p - X\lambda \geq 0, \\ & \quad I1'\lambda = 1 \\ & \quad \lambda \geq 0 \end{aligned} \tag{1}$$

where I is an $I \times 1$ vector of ones, y_i is the output q of the bank, x_i is the input p of the bank, θ is a scalar representing the efficiency score of the banks (ranging between 0 and 1), and λ is a vector of $N \times 1$ constants.

VRS decomposes the overall technical efficiency score into pure technical efficiency and scale efficiency. Pure technical efficiency deals with managerial efficiency, as it relates to the ability of managers to utilize the bank's factors of production, whereas scale efficiency is based on the concept of economies of scale, whereby the bank is assumed to gain from a larger scale of operation.

Next, the cost efficiency is specified by Equation (2).

$$
\begin{aligned}
& Min \sum_p w_{jp} x_{jp} \\
& s.t. \sum_i \lambda_i y_{iq} \geq y_{jq} \quad \forall q \\
& \quad \sum_i \lambda_i x_{ip} \geq x_{jp} \quad \forall p \\
& \quad \sum_i \lambda_i = 1; \lambda_i \geq 0; i = 1, \ldots, N
\end{aligned} \tag{2}
$$

where N firms ($i = 1,\ldots, N$) use a vector of p inputs $x_i = (x_{i1}, \ldots, x_{ip}) \in \Re_{p++}$ with the prices of inputs of $w_i = (w_{i1}, \ldots, w_{ip}) \in \Re_{p++}$ in producing a vector of q outputs $y_i = (y_{i1}, \ldots, y_{iq}) \in \Re_{q++}$ that will be sold at prices of $r_i = (r_{i1}, \ldots, r_{iq}) \in \Re_{q++}$. The solution to this system is given by $x_j^* = (x_{j1}^*, \ldots, x_{jp}^*)$, which corresponds to the input demand vector that minimizes costs for given input prices. The cost efficiency for firm j is then calculated as:

$$
CE_j = \frac{C_j^*}{C_j} = \sum_p \frac{w_{jp} x_{jp}^*}{w_{jp} x_{jp}} \tag{3}
$$

where CE_j is defined as the ratio between minimum costs (C_j^*) using the input vector (x_j^*) and observed costs (C_j) for firm j.

The standard profit function shown in Equation (4) is used to estimate the profit efficiency in this study.

$$
\begin{aligned}
& Max \sum_q r_{jq} y_{jq} - \sum_p w_{jp} x_{jp} \\
& s.t. \sum_i \lambda_i y_{iq} \geq y_{jq} \quad \forall q \\
& \quad \sum_i \lambda_i x_{ip} \geq x_{jp} \quad \forall p \\
& \quad \sum_i \lambda_i = 1; \lambda_i \geq 0; i = 1, \ldots, N
\end{aligned} \tag{4}
$$

The vector of outputs is defined as $y_j^* = (y_{j1}^*, \ldots, y_{jq}^*)$, with the input vector of $x_j^* = (x_{j1}^*, \ldots, x_{jp}^*)$ that maximizes profits with the given price of outputs r and of inputs w. The profit efficiency for firm j is then calculated as:

$$
SPE_j = \frac{P_j}{SP_j^*} = \frac{\sum_q r_{iq} y_{jq} - \sum_p w_{jp} x_{jp}}{\sum_q r_{iq} y_{jq}^* - \sum_p w_{jp} x_{jp}^*} \tag{5}
$$

Table 2.3 Price of inputs and outputs

Prices of inputs	
Price of labour	total wages and salaries/total assets
Price of physical capital	total depreciation/total fixed assets
Price of deposits	interest expenses/total deposits
Prices of outputs	
Price of loans	interest income on loan/total loans and advances
Price of investments	interest income on investment/total other earning assets
Price of off-balance-sheet items	noninterest income/total off-balance-sheet items

2.3.2 *Input and output specification*

We specify the inputs and outputs in our study on the basis of the intermediation approach proposed by Sealey and Lindley (1977). In this case, the inputs consist of labour, physical capital, and deposits, which are used to produce earning assets such as loans and investments. We further include off-balance-sheet items, such as one of the bank's outputs, because off-balance-sheet items significantly add to the sources of income of banks and should be included in the estimation for efficiency analysis (Jagtiani and Khanthavit, 1996).

For estimating cost and profit efficiencies, the prices of inputs and outputs needed in the estimation are shown in Table 2.3.

2.4 Cost, profit, and technical efficiency performances

2.4.1 *Overall performance*

In this subsection, we discuss the efficiency scores of conventional and Islamic Malaysian banks. We further analyze whether their levels of efficiency have improved or deteriorated during and after the AFC period, the merger wave, and the financial reform following the crisis period, and we compare local banks with foreign banks.

Table 2.4 indicates that the banks are better off in terms of technical efficiency – that is, the ability of the banks to manipulate its factors of production, such as labour, capital, and deposits, in order to generate a given level of output. The average score reported for technical efficiency is 84.19%, as compared to 79.16% and 48.99% for profit efficiency and cost efficiency, respectively. We found that banks were on average inferior in

Table 2.4 Efficiency scores of Malaysian commercial banks

Year	*Profit efficiency*	*Cost efficiency*	*Technical efficiency*
2000	0.7454	0.6366	0.8457
2001	0.7717	0.6430	0.8158
2002	0.7946	0.6475	0.8428
2003	0.8330	0.7935	0.9006
2004	0.8135	0.6961	0.8967
2005	0.8657	0.6280	0.9040
2006	0.8062	0.3358	0.8449
2007	0.8026	0.3944	0.8817
2008	0.7904	0.4336	0.8544
2009	0.8119	0.5222	0.8718
2010	0.6205	0.4173	0.7031
2011	0.6679	0.4335	0.7199
2012	0.7931	0.4137	0.8381
2013	0.8328	0.3776	0.8403
2014	0.8580	0.3183	0.8953
2015	0.8141	0.3170	0.8244
2016	0.8363	0.3201	0.8336
Average Score	0.7916	0.4899	0.8419
FSMP I (2001–2005)	0.8157	0.6816	0.8720
FSMP I (2006–2010)	0.8312	0.4207	0.7663
FSMP II (2011–2016)	0.8253	0.3633	0.8004

terms of cost efficiency, with an average score of 48.99%. This means that banks fail to utilize the factors of production by taking into account their respective prices. In this case, banks can further reduce their resources by 51.01% in order to be cost-efficient.

Looking at year-to-year performances, we see that the commercial banks began to experience deterioration in terms of the cost efficiency value of 33.58%. This may due to increases in the price of factors of production that make banks relatively inefficient in allocating their resources to the best use. We found that the cost efficiency decreased to 31.70% in 2015. This may be due to the sharp increase in the price of inputs, due to the effects following the implementation of the Goods and Services Tax (GST), which was fully enacted in April 2015.

The relatively low cost efficiency found in the Malaysian banking industry is consistent with the traditional measure of bank efficiency using bank

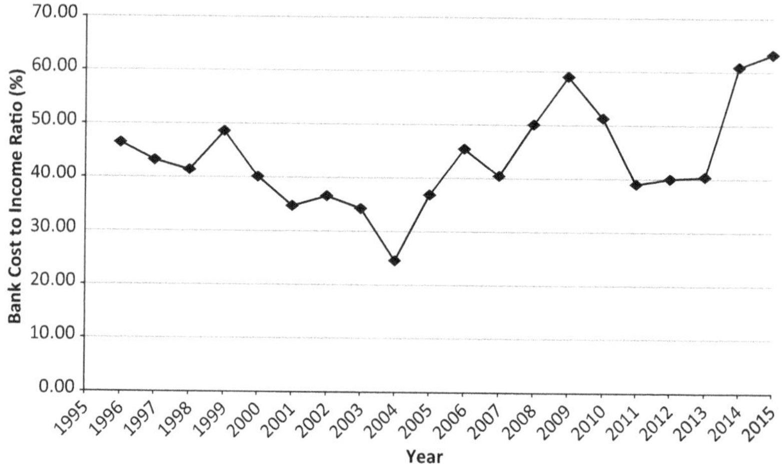

Figure 2.12 Bank cost-to-income ratio (%)

cost to income ratio, as indicated by Figure 2.12. This shows that the bank cost-to-income ratio has increased gradually since 2005. This is consistent with the decrease in cost efficiency in Table 2.4 since year 2005. The relatively low cost efficiency since 2005 may due to the increase in the price of capital at a rate of 8% per annum, which consists of a significant portion of the banking assets, as measured by the fixed assets of the banks in the production of financial product and services.

On the other hand, profit efficiency dropped to its lowest value in 2008, with an average of 79.04%. This may be due to the decrease in the sales of financial products and services that result from the impact of GFC. The technical efficiency of the commercial banks is relatively stable over time, indicating that commercial banks are stable in resource allocation after the pricing of inputs and outputs has been factored out. The results further indicate that the commercial banks need to pay more attention to cost control. Hence, policy makers and bank management should focus on how to minimize the cost of the banking operation in order to increase the banks' efficiency and improve the long-term survivability of the banking system in Malaysia.

Next, we examine the effectiveness of the FSMP I and II policies and the measures taken to improve overall bank performance. To achieve this, we have segregated the efficiency scores into three sub periods, with a Phase 1 (2000–2005) and a Phase 2 (2006–2010) during the FSMP I, and a Phase 1 (2011–2016) during the FSMP II. Table 2.4 shows a more stable profit efficiency performance for the three sub periods, where Malaysian banks tended to be at more than 80% of their greatest profit efficiency level.

In terms of technical performance, these banks operated at an outstanding 87% technical efficiency in Phase 1 of FSMP I. However, these banks were unable to maintain the technical efficiency level above 80%, and it dropped to 77% in Phase 2. Fortunately, the banks were able to rebound their technical efficiency to 80% in Phase 1 of FSMP II. A contrary performance was displayed for cost efficiency, which deteriorated from Phase 1 in FSMP I to Phase 1 in FSMP II. This statistic confirms that Malaysian banks were at 68% of their greatest level of cost efficiency in Phase 1 of FSMP I, and dramatically reduced to only 42% in Phase 2; it continued to fall to 36% in Phase 1 of FSMP I.

The evidence suggests that, among domestic banks, the policies and measures implemented in FSMP I and FSMP II were only translated into better profit and technical efficiency, and not cost efficiency. In the near future, policy makers and regulators need to diagnose and identify the best alternative strategy in Phase 2 (FSMP II), which will end in 2020, to enhance cost efficiency performance and avoid further deterioration in cost performance among banks.

2.4.2 Comparison of Islamic and conventional banks

We further examine the efficiency scores by type of bank, conventional or Islamic, to see whether bank performance is affected by the nature of the banking operation, which in conventional banks and Islamic banks is governed by different types of regulations and principals.

The two-sample *t*-test was performed to further verify whether the performance values of the conventional and Islamic banks were statistically significant in terms of technical efficiency, cost efficiency, and profit efficiency. We ran the *F*-test for equal variances before running the two-sample *t*-test to determine the assumption underlying the two-sample *t*-test to be employed. Based on the results presented in Table 2.6, we used the two-sample *t*-test with unequal variance to determine the significant different between conventional and Islamic banks, whereas equal variances were assumed for profit efficiency.

In Table 2.5, the efficiency performances have been divided between Islamic and conventional Malaysia banks according to the three sub periods of FSMP I and FSMP II. The results show that Islamic banks tended to outperform the conventional banks in profit efficiency performance during Phase 1 of FSMP I. The Islamic banks were at 92% of their best profit efficiency, while the conventional banks were at 85%. However, the conventional banks overtook the Islamic banks in Phase 1 of FSMP II.

Table 2.5 Efficiency scores for conventional and Islamic Malaysian banks

Year	*Profit efficiency*		*Cost efficiency*		*Technical efficiency*	
	Conventional banks	*Islamic banks*	*Conventional banks*	*Islamic banks*	*Conventional banks*	*Islamic banks*
2000	0.7654	1.0000	0.6383	0.7964	0.7654	1.0000
2001	0.7869	1.0000	0.6426	0.6590	0.7869	1.0000
2002	0.8258	0.9554	0.6555	0.5878	0.8258	0.8434
2003	0.8611	1.0000	0.7943	0.6187	0.8611	1.0000
2004	0.8692	0.8339	0.8331	0.5553	0.8692	0.7949
2005	0.8870	0.8974	0.8181	0.9623	0.8870	0.9469
2006	0.8505	0.9369	0.4717	0.7721	0.8505	0.9202
2007	0.8758	0.8934	0.5233	0.4620	0.8758	0.8739
2008	0.8830	0.9466	0.4390	0.6896	0.8830	0.9380
2009	0.8522	0.9768	0.7748	0.5709	0.8522	0.9630
2010	0.8647	0.6374	0.7760	0.4484	0.8647	0.6117
2011	0.8730	0.6628	0.7353	0.4782	0.8730	0.6753
2012	0.8792	0.9275	0.7919	0.4654	0.8792	0.9084
2013	0.9039	0.9520	0.7493	0.4385	0.9039	0.9471
2014	0.9803	0.9735	0.7167	0.3873	0.9803	0.9704
2015	0.9316	0.8542	0.6629	0.4058	0.9316	0.8656
2016	0.9647	0.8737	0.8023	0.4436	0.9647	0.8834
Average Score	0.8806	0.8839	0.6992	0.5590	0.8951	0.9151
FSMP I (2001–2005)	0.8460	0.9170	0.7487	0.6766	0.8917	0.9373
FSMP I (2006–2010)	0.8652	0.8614	0.5970	0.5886	0.9087	0.8782
FSMP II (2011–2016)	0.9221	0.8750	0.7431	0.4365	0.9401	0.8739

Table 2.6 Two-sample *t*-test between conventional and Islamic banks

	Two-sample t-statistics	F-*test for equal variances*
Technical efficiency	1.9319**	2.2132***
Cost efficiency	5.5286***	2.2329***
Profit efficiency	0.0630	1.1119

*/**/*** denotes significance level to 10%/5%/1%, respectively

Comparing technical efficiency performance, a small reduction was exhibited for Islamic banks for the three sub periods, and vice versa for conventional banks. The Islamic banks were likely to be at their highest technical efficiency of 94% in Phase 1 of FSMP I, while the conventional banks were at 94% in Phase 1 of FSMP II. In addition, the Islamic banks were at a slight low of 87% of their technical efficiency in Phase 1 of FSMP II, while the conventional banks were at 89% in Phase 1 of FSMP I.

When we compared the cost efficiency performances of Islamic banks with those of conventional banks during the three similar sub periods, we found that the root cause of the extreme deterioration in the overall cost efficiency was due to Islamic banks' worst performance, rather than the conventional banks'. The significant fall in cost efficiency among Islamic banks further squeezed the overall cost efficiency for the three sub periods (Table 2.5).

In general, the results in Table 2.5 suggest that these banks were better off in terms of technical efficiency, followed by profit efficiency and cost efficiency, for the period 2000–2016. The Islamic banks were superior in terms of technical efficiency and profit efficiency, with average scores of 91.51% and 88.39%, respectively. On the other hand, the conventional banks were better off in terms of cost efficiency, with an average score of 69.92%, as compared to 55.90% for the Islamic banks.

The differences in cost efficiency between the conventional banks and Islamic banks are statistically significant at the 1% significance level. Consistent with previous studies, such as those of Abdul-Majid, Nor and Said (2005) and Kamaruddin, Safad and Mohd (2008), we found that the Islamic banks performed better in terms of cost efficiency in the earlier years. We observed that the relatively low cost efficiency scores of the Islamic banks are due to the decrease in cost efficiency since 2009. This is consistent with the findings of Samad (2004), who found that Islamic banks performed as efficiently as conventional banks, though not for cost efficiency (Iqbal, 2001; Hassan, 2005). The cost efficiency score dropped on average from 57.09% in 2009 to 44.36% in 2016. This decrease should not be overlooked, as it may indicate complacency in managing the cost of banking operations. The management should therefore focus on policies to better control costs in order to provide long-term sustainability to Islamic banks and to further expand the operation of the Islamic banks that are emerging in the country.

Similar to Willison (2009) and Yilmaz (2009), we also found that the performance of Islamic banks was not affected by the GFC. This can be seen by the relatively stable increase in profit efficiency and technical efficiency from 2010 to 2016. The differences between conventional banks and Islamic banks in terms of technical efficiency are statistically significant at the 5% significance level. This may be because the Islamic banks are highly regulated by nature, since they must be strictly Shariah compliant in their operations. Less speculative and less risky investments may have led to relatively stable earnings during the GFC, which further improved the profit efficiency of Islamic banks in recent years. These results are consistent with the study of Sufian (2010), who also found that Malaysian Islamic banks tended to be more profitable; the explanation suggested for this is that Islamic banks are said to work more in partnership, joint ventures, and sales, thus increasing profitability despite high-risk (Rosly and Bakar, 2003).

References

Journal articles

Abdul-Majid, M., Md. Nor, N.G., and Said, F.F. (2005). Efficiency of Islamic banks in Malaysia. In Munawar Iqbal and Ausaf Ahmed (Eds.), *Islamic Finance and Economic Development* (pp. 94–115). New York: Palgrave Macmillan.

Abdul-Majid, M., Saal, D.S., and Battisti, G. (2010). Efficiency in Islamic and conventional banking: An international comparison. *Journal of Productivity Analysis, 34*(1), 25–43.

Al-Muharrami, S. (2008). An examination of technical, pure technical and scale efficiencies in GCC banking. *American Journal of Finance and Accounting, 1*(2), 152–166.

Alpay, S., and Hassan, M.K. (2007, November). A comparative efficiency analysis of interest-free financial institutions and conventional banks: A case study on Turkey. In *Economic Research Forum*. Working Paper No. 0714, 1–18.

Alshammari, S.H. (2003). *Structure-Conduct-Performance and Efficiency in Gulf Co-operation Council*. PhD thesis, University of Wales, Bangor.

Al-Sharkas, A.A., Hassan, M.K., and Lawrence, S. (2008). The impact of mergers and acquisitions on the efficiency of the US banking industry: Further evidence. *Journal of Business Finance and Accounting, 35*(1–2), 50–70.

Aly, H.Y., Grabowski, R., Pasurka, C., and Rangan, N. (1990). Technical, scale, and allocative efficiencies in US banking: An empirical investigation. *The Review of Economics and Statistics, 72*(2), 211–218.

Ataullah, A., Cockerill, T., and Le, H. (2004). Financial liberalization and bank efficiency: A comparative analysis of India and Pakistan. *Applied Economics, 36*(17), 1915–1924.

Athukorala, P.C. (2010). Malaysian economy in three crises. Working paper in trade and development. Working Paper No. 2010/12.

Bader, M.K.I., Mohamad, S., Ariff, M., and Hassan, T. (2008). Cost, revenue and profit efficiency of Islamic versus conventional banks: International evidence using data envelopment analysis. *Islamic Economic Studies, 15*(2), 23–72.

Banker, R.D., Charnes, A., and Cooper, W.W. (1984). Some models for estimating technical and scale inefficiencies in data envelopment analysis. *Management Science, 30*, 1078–1092.

Battellino, R. (2010, March). Mining booms and the Australian economy. *RBA Bulletin*, 63–69.

Beck, T., Demirguc-Kunt, A., Levine, R.E., Cihak, M., and Feyen, E.H.B. (2015). Financial development and structure dataset. The World Bank. Retreived from http://www.worldbank.org/en/publication/gfdr/data/financial-structure-database

Berg, S.A., Forsund, F.R., Hjalmarsson, L., and Souminen, M. (1993). Banking efficiency in Nordic countries. *Journal of Banking and Finance, 17*, 371–388.

Bhattacharya, A., Lovell, C.A.K., and Sahay, P. (1997). The impact of liberalization on the productive efficiency of Indian commercial banks. *European Journal of Operational Research, 98*, 332–345.

Burki, A.A., and Niazi, G.S.K. (2010). Impact of financial reforms on efficiency of state-owned, private and foreign banks in Pakistan. *Applied Economics, 42*(24), 3147–3160.

Chang, T.C., and Chiu, Y.H. (2006). Affecting factors on risk-adjusted efficiency in Taiwan's banking industry. *Contemporary Economic Policy, 24*(4), 634–648.

Chapra, U. (2003). International financial stability: The role of Islamic finance. *Policy Perspectives, 4*(2), 91–113.

Charnes, A., Cooper, W.W., and Rhodes, E. (1978). Measuring the efficiency of decision making units. *European Journal of Operational Research, 2*, 429–444.

Chen, T.Y. (2004). A study of cost efficiency and privatisation in Taiwan's banks: The impact of the Asian financial crisis. *Service Industries Journal, 24*(5), 137–151.

Claessens, S., Demirgüç-Kunt, A., and Huizinga, H. (2001). How does foreign entry affect domestic banking markets? *Journal of Banking and Finance, 25*(5), 891–911.

Das, A., and Kumbhakar, S.C. (2012). Productivity and efficiency dynamics in Indian banking: An input distance function approach incorporating quality of inputs and outputs. *Journal of Applied Econometrics, 27*(2), 205–234.

Das, A., Nag, A., and Ray, S.C. (2005). Liberalisation, ownership and efficiency in Indian banking: A nonparametric analysis. *Economic and Political Weekly, 40*(12), 1190–1197.

Drake, L., Hall, M.J., and Simper, R. (2006). The impact of macroeconomic and regulatory factors on bank efficiency: A non-parametric analysis of Hong Kong's banking system. *Journal of Banking & Finance, 30*(5), 1443–1466.

El-Gamal, M.A., and Inanoglu, H. (2005). Inefficiency and heterogeneity in Turkish banking: 1990–2000. *Journal of Applied Econometrics, 20*(5), 641–664.

Elyasiani, E., Mehdian, S., and Rezvanian, R. (1994). An empirical test of association between production and financial performance: The case of the commercial banking industry. *Applied Financial Economics, 4*(1), 55–60.

Erdem, C., and Erdem, M.S. (2008). Turkish banking efficiency and its relation to stock performance. *Applied Economics Letters, 15*(3), 207–211.

Fang, Y., Hasan, I., and Marton, K. (2011). Bank efficiency in South-Eastern Europe. *Economics of Transition, 19*(3), 495–520.

Favero, C.A., and Papi, L. (1995). Technical efficiency and scale efficiency in the Italian banking sector: A non-parametric approach. *Applied Economics, 27*(4), 385–395.

Ferrier, G.D., and Lovell, C.K. (1990). Measuring cost efficiency in banking: Econometric and linear programming evidence. *Journal of Econometrics, 46*(1–2), 229–245.

Figueira, C., Nellis, J., and Parker, D. (2009). The effects of ownership on bank efficiency in Latin America. *Applied Economics, 41*(18), 2353–2368.

Focarelli, D., Panetta, F., and Salleo, C. (2002). Why do banks merge? *Journal of Money, Credit, and Banking, 34*(4), 1047–1066.

Gardener, E., Molyneux, P., and Nguyen-Linh, H. (2011). Determinants of efficiency in South East Asian banking. *Service Industries Journal, 31*(16), 2693–2719.

Gilbert, R.A., and Wilson, P.W. (1998). Effects of deregulation on the productivity of Korean banks. *Journal of Economics and Business, 50*(2), 133–155.

Girardone, C., Molyneux, P., and Gardener, E.P. (2004). Analysing the determinants of bank efficiency: The case of Italian banks. *Applied Economics, 36*(3), 215–227.

Guzman, I., and Reverte, C. (2008). Productivity and efficiency change and shareholder value: Evidence from the Spanish banking sector. *Applied Economics, 40*(15), 2037–2044.

Hassan, M.K. (2005). The cost, profit and X-efficiency of Islamic banks. *Economic Research Forum 12th Annual Conference,* Cairo, Egypt.

Hassan, M.K. (2006). The X-efficiency in Islamic banks. *Islamic Economic Studies, 13*, 50–78.

Hassan, T., Mohamad, S., Khaled I., and Bader, M. (2009). Efficiency of conventional versus Islamic banks: Evidence from the Middle East. *International Journal of Islamic and Middle Eastern Finance and Management, 2*(1), 46–65.

Havidz, S.A.H., and Setiawan, C. (2015). Bank efficiency and non-performing financing (NPF) in the Indonesian Islamic banks. *Asian Journal of Economic Modelling, 3*(3), 61–79.

Hellmann, T.F., Murdock, K.C., and Stiglitz, J.E. (2000). Liberalization, moral hazard in banking, and prudential regulation: Are capital requirements enough? *American Economic Review*, 147–165.

Hermes, N., and Meesters, A. (2015). Financial liberalization, financial regulation and bank efficiency: A multi-country analysis. *Applied Economics, 47*(21), 2154–2172.

Hermes, N., and Nhung, V.T.H. (2010). The impact of financial liberalization on bank efficiency: Evidence from Latin America and Asia. *Applied Economics, 42*(26), 3351–3365.

Hu, J.L., Li, Y., and Chiu, Y.H. (2004). Ownership and nonperforming loans: Evidence from Taiwan's banks. *The Developing Economies, 42*(3), 405–420.

Iqbal, M. (2001). Islamic and conventional banking in the nineties: A comparative study. *Islamic Economic Studies, 8*(2), 1–27.

Jagtiani, J., and Khanthavit, A. (1996). Scale and scope economies at large banks: Including off-balance sheet products and regulatory effects (1984–1991). *Journal of Banking and Finance, 20*, 1271–1287.

Johnes, J., Izzeldin, M., and Pappas, V. (2014). A comparison of performance of Islamic and conventional banks 2004–2009. *Journal of Economic Behavior & Organization, 103*, S93–S107.

Jonas, M.R., and King, S.K. (2008). Bank efficiency and the effectiveness of monetary policy. *Contemporary Economic Policy, 26*(4), 579–589.

Kamaruddin, B.H., Safab, M.S., and Mohd, R. (2008). Assessing production efficiency of Islamic banks and conventional bank Islamic windows in Malaysia. *International Journal of Business and Management Science, 1*(1), 31.

Karim, M.Z.A. (2001). Comparative bank efficiency across select ASEAN countries. *ASEAN Economic Bulletin*, 289–304.

Kasman, A., and Yildirim, C. (2006). Cost and profit efficiencies in transition banking: The case of new EU members. *Applied Economics, 38*(9), 1079–1090.

Kaur, B.P., and Kaur, G. (2010). Impact of mergers on the cost efficiency of Indian commercial banks. *Eurasian Journal of Business and Economics, 3*(5), 27–50.

Kohers, T., Huang, M.H., and Kohers, N. (2000). Market perception of efficiency in bank holding company mergers: The roles of the DEA and SFA models in capturing merger potential. *Review of Financial Economics, 9*(2), 101–120.

Kraft, E., Hofler, R., and Payne, J. (2006). Privatization, foreign bank entry and bank efficiency in Croatia: A Fourier-flexible function stochastic cost frontier analysis. *Applied Economics, 38*(17), 2075–2088.

Krishnasamy, G., Hanuum Ridzwa, A., and Perumal, V. (2004). Malaysian post merger banks' productivity: Application of Malmquist productivity index. *Managerial Finance, 30*(4), 63–74.

Lehner, M., and Schnitzer, M. (2008). Entry of foreign banks and their impact on host countries. *Journal of Comparative Economics, 36*(3), 430–452.

Levine, R. (1996). Foreign banks, financial development, and economic growth. In E.B. Claude (Ed.), *International Financial Markets*. Washington, DC: AEI Press.

Matthews, K., and Ismail, M. (2006). Efficiency and productivity growth of domestic and foreign commercial banks in Malaysia. Working Paper, Cardiff University, UK.

McAllister, P.H., and McManus, D. (1993). Resolving the scale efficiency puzzle in banking. *Journal of Banking & Finance, 17*(2–3), 389–405.

Miller, S.M., and Noulas, A.G. (1996). The technical efficiency of large bank production. *Journal of Banking & Finance, 20*(3), 495–509.

Mishkin, F.S., and Strahan, P.E. (1999). What will technology do to the financial structure? In R. Litan and A. Santomero (Eds.), *The Effect of Technology on the Financial Sector* (pp. 249–287). Brookings-Wharton Papers on Financial Services. Hamphire, UK: Palgrave Macmillan.

Mobarek, A., and Kalonov, A. (2014). Comparative performance analysis between conventional and Islamic banks: Empirical evidence from OIC countries. *Applied Economics, 46*(3), 253–270.

Mohan, T.R., and Ray, S.C. (2004). Comparing performance of public and private sector banks: A revenue maximisation efficiency approach. *Economic and Political Weekly, 39*(12), 1271–1276.

Mokhtar, H.S.A., Abdullah, N., and Al-Habshi, S.M. (2006). Efficiency of Islamic banking in Malaysia: A stochastic frontier approach. *Journal of Economic Cooperation, 27*(2), 37–70.

Mokhtar, H.S.A., Abdullah, N., and Al-Habshi, S.M. (2008). Efficiency and competition of Islamic banking in Malaysia. *Humanomics, 24*(1), 28–48.

Olson, D., and Zoubi, T.A. (2008). Using accounting ratios to distinguish between Islamic and conventional banks in the GCC region. *The International Journal of Accounting, 43*(1), 45–65.

Pasiouras, F. (2008). International evidence on the impact of regulations and supervision on banks' technical efficiency: An application of two-stage data envelopment analysis. *Review of Quantitative Finance and Accounting, 30*, 187–223.

Paul, S., and Kourouche, K. (2008). Regulatory policy and the efficiency of the banking sector in Australia. *Australian Economic Review, 41*(3), 260–271.

Peng, Y.H., and Wang, K. (2004). Cost efficiency and the effect of mergers on the Taiwanese banking industry. *The Service Industries Journal, 24*(4), 21–39.

Piloff, S.J., and Santomero, A.M. (1998). The value effects of bank mergers and acquisitions. In *Bank Mergers and Acquisitions* (pp. 59–78). Boston: Springer.

Poghosyan, T., and Poghosyan, A. (2010). Foreign bank entry, bank efficiency and market power in Central and Eastern European countries. *Economics of Transition, 18*(3), 571–598.

Poshakwale, S.S., and Qian, B. (2011). Competitiveness and efficiency of the banking sector and economic growth in Egypt. *African Development Review, 23*(1), 99–120.

Rahim, S.R.M. (2015). How efficient are Islamic banks in Malaysia? *Journal of Business Studies Quarterly, 6*(3), 164.

Rahman, A.R.A., and Rosman, R. (2013). Efficiency of Islamic banks: A comparative analysis of MENA and Asian countries. *Journal of Economic Cooperation & Development, 34*(1), 63.

Řepková, I. (2015). Banking efficiency determinants in the Czech banking sector. *Procedia Economics and Finance, 23*, 191–196.

Rosly, S.A., and Bakar, M.A.A. (2003). Performance of Islamic and mainstream banks in Malaysia. *International Journal of Social Economics, 20*, 1249–1265.

Samad, A. (2004). Performance of interest-free Islamic banks vis-à-vis interest-based conventional banks of Bahrain. *International Journal of Economics, Management and Accounting, 12*(2).

Schularick, M., and Taylor, A.M. (2012). Credit booms gone bust: Monetary policy, leverage cycles, and financial crises, 1870–2008. *American Economic Review, 102*(2), 1029–1061.

Sealey, C.W., Jr., and Lindley, J.T. (1977). Inputs, outputs and a theory of production and cost at depository financial institutions. *Journal of Finance, 32*, 1251–1266.

Sensarma, R. (2005). Cost and profit efficiency of Indian banks during 1986–2003: A stochastic frontier analysis. *Economic and Political Weekly, XL*(12), 1198–1209.

Srairi, S.A. (2010). Cost and profit efficiency of conventional and Islamic banks in GCC countries. *Journal of Productivity Analysis, 34*(1), 45–62.

Srinivasan, A., and Wall, L.D. (1992). Cost savings associated with bank mergers. Working Paper No. 92–2, Federal Reserve Bank of Atlanta.

Stewart, C., Matousek, R., and Nguyen, T.N. (2016). Efficiency in the Vietnamese banking system: A DEA double bootstrap approach. *Research in International Business and Finance, 36*, 96–111.

Sturm, J.E., and Williams, B. (2004). Foreign bank entry, deregulation and bank efficiency: Lessons from the Australian experience. *Journal of Banking and Finance, 28*(7), 1775–1799.

Sufian, F. (2007). The efficiency of Islamic banking industry in Malaysia: Foreign vs domestic banks. *Humanomics, 23*(3), 174–192.

Sufian, F. (2009). Determinants of bank profitability in a developing economy: Empirical evidence from the china banking sector. *Journal of Asia-Pacific Business, 10*, 281–307.

Sufian, F. (2010). Does foreign presence foster Islamic banks' performance? Empirical evidence from Malaysia. *Journal of Islamic Accounting and Business Research, 1*(2), 128–147.

Sufian, F., and Habibullah, M.S. (2009). Bank specific and macroeconomic determinants of bank profitability: Empirical evidence from the China banking sector. *Frontiers of Economics in China, 4*(2), 274–291.

Sufian, F., and Kamarudin, F. (2015). Determinants of revenue efficiency of Islamic banks: Empirical evidence from the Southeast Asian countries. *International Journal of Islamic and Middle Eastern Finance and Management, 8*(1), 36–63.

Sun, L., and Chang, T.P. (2011). A comprehensive analysis of the effects of risk measures on bank efficiency: Evidence from emerging Asian countries. *Journal of Banking and Finance, 35*(7), 1727–1735.

Thanassoulis, E. (2001). *Introduction to the Theory and Application of Data Envelopment Analysis: A Foundation Text with Integrated Software*. New York: Kluwer Academic.

Thoraneenitiyan, N., and Avkiran, N.K. (2009). Measuring the impact of restructuring and country-specific factors on the efficiency of post-crisis East Asian banking systems: Integrating DEA with SFA. *Socio-Economic Planning Sciences, 43*(4), 240–252.

Tsionas, E.G., Assaf, A.G., and Matousek, R. (2015). Dynamic technical and allocative efficiencies in European banking. *Journal of Banking and Finance, 52*, 130–139.

Turk Ariss, R. (2008). Financial liberalization and bank efficiency: Evidence from post-war Lebanon. *Applied Financial Economics, 18*(11), 931–946.

Uhde, A., and Heimeshoff, U. (2009). Consolidation in banking and financial stability in Europe: Empirical evidence. *Journal of Banking and Finance, 33*(7), 1299–1311.

Vu, H.T., and Turnell, S. (2010). Cost efficiency of the banking sector in Vietnam: A Bayesian stochastic frontier approach with regularity constraints. *Asian Economic Journal, 24*(2), 115–139.

Wheelock, D.C., and Wilson, P.W. (1995). Explaining bank failures: Deposit insurance, regulation, and efficiency. *The Review of Economics and Statistics, 77*(4), 689–700.

Williams, J., and Nguyen, N. (2005). Financial liberalisation, crisis, and restructuring: A comparative study of bank performance and bank governance in South East Asia. *Journal of Banking and Finance, 29*(8), 2119–2154.

Willison, B. (2009). ETechnology trends in Islamic investment banking. *Islamic Finance News, 6*(19).

Wu, Y.C., Ting, I.W.K., Lu, W.M., Nourani, M., and Kweh, Q.L. (2016). The impact of earnings management on the performance of ASEAN banks. *Economic Modelling, 53*, 156–165.

Yao, S., Jiang, C., Feng, G., and Willenbockel, D. (2007). WTO challenges and efficiency of Chinese banks. *Applied Economics, 39*(5), 629–643.

Yildirim, I. (2015). Financial differences and similarities of Islamic banks: A study on Qismut countries. *Journal of Business Economics and Finance, 4*(2).

Yılmaz, D. (2009). Governor of the Central Bank of the Republic of Turkey. Speech at the conference on "Islamic Finance–During and After the Global Financial Crisis." IMF-World Bank Annual Meetings.

Yudistira, D. (2004). Efficiency in Islamic banking: An empirical analysis of eighteen banks. *Islamic Economic Studies*, *12*(1), 1–19.

Yusoff, M.B., Hasan, F.A., and Jalil, S.A. (2000). Globalisation, economic policy and equity: The case of Malaysia. *Poverty and Income Inequality in Developing Countries: A Policy Dialogue on the Effects of Globalisation* (OECD Development Centre Paper), 1–81.

Zhang, X., and Daly, K. (2014). The impact of bank-specific and macroeconomic factors on China's bank performance. *Chinese Economy*, *47*(5–6), 5–28.

List of reports

Bank Negara Malaysia Annual Report 1998. Retrieved from www.bnm.gov.my/index.php?ch=en_publication&pg=en_ar&ac=3&lang=en

Bank Negara Malaysia Annual Report 1999. Retrieved from www.bnm.gov.my/index.php?ch=en_publication&pg=en_ar&ac=3&lang=en

Bank Negara Malaysia Annual Report 2000. Retrieved from www.bnm.gov.my/index.php?ch=en_publication&pg=en_ar&ac=3&lang=en

Bank Negara Malaysia Annual Report 2001. Retrieved from www.bnm.gov.my/index.php?ch=en_publication&pg=en_ar&ac=3&lang=en

Bank Negara Malaysia Annual Report 2002. Retrieved from www.bnm.gov.my/index.php?ch=en_publication&pg=en_ar&ac=3&lang=en

Bank Negara Malaysia Annual Report 2003. Retrieved from www.bnm.gov.my/index.php?ch=en_publication&pg=en_ar&ac=3&lang=en

Bank Negara Malaysia Annual Report 2004. Retrieved from www.bnm.gov.my/index.php?ch=en_publication&pg=en_ar&ac=3&lang=en

Bank Negara Malaysia Annual Report 2009. Retrieved from www.bnm.gov.my/index.php?ch=en_publication&pg=en_ar&ac=3&lang=en

Bank Negara Malaysia Annual Report 2010. Retrieved from www.bnm.gov.my/index.php?ch=en_publication&pg=en_ar&ac=3&lang=en

Bank Negara Malaysia Annual Report 2012. Retrieved from www.bnm.gov.my/index.php?ch=en_publication&pg=en_ar&ac=3&lang=en

Bank Negara Malaysia Annual Report 2017. Retrieved from http://www.bnm.gov.my/index.php?ch=li&cat=islamic&type=IB&fund=0&cu=0

Financial Sector Blueprint 2011–2020. Retrieved from www.bnm.gov.my/index.php?ch=en_publication&pg=en_fsmp&ac=7&en

Financial Sector Masterplan 2001–2010. Retrieved from www.bnm.gov.my/index.php?ch=en_publication&pg=en_fsmp&ac=7&en

Islamic Financial Services Industry Stability Report 2013. Retrieved from www.ifsb.org/docs/IFSIpercent20Stabilitypercent20Reportpercent202016percent20(final).pdf

Islamic Financial Services Industry Stability Report 2016. Retrieved from www.ifsb.org/docs/IFSIpercent20Stabilitypercent20Reportpercent202016percent20(final).pdf

Malaysian Islamic Financial Report 2015. Retrieved from www.irti.org/English/News/Documents/406.pd)

3 Bank risk management

Rozaimah Zainudin, Chan Sok-Gee, and Aidil Rizal Shahrin

3.1 Evolution of bank risk management in Malaysian banks

3.1.1 Type of bank risk

In recent decades, several global economic crises have occurred, such as the industrial crisis in the 1980s, the Asian financial crisis (AFC) in 1997, and the recent mortgage subprime crises in 2007, which spilled over to the liquidity crisis among European banks and the 2008 global financial crisis (GFC). Ineffective bank risk management activities were the main cause of the crisis in the 1980s, as well as of the financial crises in recent years. These crises have severely affected banks, with the economic turbulence resulting in insolvency at many firms, leading to an increase in the amount of nonperforming loans. Enormous defaults in loan repayments have further led to low liquidity at banks, squeezing the banks' ability roll the loan repayment over into new loanable funds. This scenario affects the performance of banks, which should serve as financial intermediaries, further impeding payment systems in an economy. Banks are commonly associated with risky activities, and this risk can be categorized into six types: credit risk, market risk, liquidity risk, counterparty risk, legal risk, and operational risk (Santomero, 1997), described as follows:

i) Credit risk is the most common type of risk to banks, as the main activities of banks involve using the supply of loanable funds (from, for example, depositors) to satisfy the demand of borrowers. Such credit risk derives from borrowers defaulting on repayments. This is also the risk that receives the most attention from banking authorities.
ii) Market risk involves changes in banks' asset values due to the economic climate, such as adverse movement in financial markets and prices (Hendricks and Hirtle, 1997). This type of risk is also known as

systematic risk, and prevents banks from minimizing the volatility of interest rate and foreign currency movement.

iii) Santomero (1997) describes liquidity risk as lying at the root of bank funding crises. Diamond and Rajan (2001) highlight the importance of managing liquidity risk over time: banks need to ensure they have sufficient buffers to meet the extraordinary demand on depositors' funds, especially during the crisis period. They also need to address the fact that loans tend to be illiquid and payment collection thus longer. Banks then need to provide a safety net to meet unexpected seasonal liquidity needs, such as additional capital to finance investment and operational needs, which are especially important during crisis periods.

iv) Similar to credit risk, counterparty risk arises from non-performance of banks' trading partners due to unfavourable price movement attributable to market risk situations such as economic recessions, unstable political situations, and so on. Non-performance among banks' trading partners is due to factors other than credit problems.

v) Legal risk is described as the policies or laws introduced by a government which affect banking activities, such as tax regulation, environmental regulation, and so on.

vi) Operational risk arises from in-house accuracy problems during the banks' day-to-day activities, such as deposit and loan processing, system downtime, compliance with central banks, internal regulations, and external factors that lead to banks losing money (Basel Committee for Banking Supervision, 2001). External events may also lead to internal operational inefficiency – for example, when an electricity blackout leads to faults in bank systems. Even one hour's system fault can lead to huge monetary losses for banks unable to process their customers' transactions.

3.1.2 Basel I: Malaysian bank policies and practices

Central banks and individual banks need to collaboratively ensure these six types of risk are minimized, especially during periods of economic recession. An international capital adequacy accord standard was introduced by the Basel Committee for Banking Supervision in 1988 to prevent banks taking excessive risk-taking activities. This international standard aims to provide strict monitoring of banks' credit risk exposure by introducing minimal capital requirement through a risk-weighted capital ratio. Under this Basel I capital adequacy framework, risk weights of 0%, 20%, 50%, and 100% are assigned to four different asset classifications. The Malaysian central bank, Bank Negara Malaysia (BNM), has extended the asset weight classification to categories namely: 0% for cash and certain government investments, 10% for Cagarmas and Cagarmas-type debt securities, 20% for securities issued by the government and state governments, 35% for most mortgages and residential properties, 50% for other mortgages and residential properties, and 100% for all other claims – such as corporate bonds, BB-unrated bonds, etc. (Capital Adequacy Framework [Capital Components], 2018). According to the accord, a minimum of 8% of the risk-weighted capital ratio is required for every financial institution (BNM Annual Report, 1999).

Apart from credit risk, the 1996 Basel I framework introduced additional risk regulations requiring all financial institutions to include the market risk element in the capital adequacy framework. In tandem with these new regulations, BNM imposed an additional requirement that all Malaysian banks need to include interest rate and foreign-exchange-related derivative contracts exposure in their credit risk assessment from June 1997 (BNM Annual Report, 1999). This is necessary because the banking industry is exposed to extreme volatility through interest rates and foreign exchange rates. Banks thus tend to use derivative contracts to minimize unfavourable movement due to interest rates and foreign exchange rates. These derivative contracts are heavily used by banks, so it is essential to consider banks' exposure to them if we are to accurately assess the overall risk exposure of individual banks at any point in time. An accurate estimation of risk exposure is crucial in ensuring the readiness of banks to absorb shocks from the market.

According to BNM (1999), domestic banks that have weaker credit risk management were badly affected during the AFC in 1997. Their weak risk management resulted in less accurate credit risk assessment and they tended to overestimate or underestimate their real credit exposure. When the currency crisis hit Malaysia in 1997, many firms declared bankruptcy and the negative effects were transmitted to the banking sector, as banks needed to absorb large amounts of nonperforming loans. Based on the risk-weighted capital ratio in Table 3.1, many Malaysian banks maintained their RWCR above the minimum 8% requirement of Basel I. The RWCR of the overall banking system was recorded at 10.6% in 1996 and dropped slightly to 10.5% in 1997. However, the ratio continued to increase from 11.8% to 12.4% in the two years after the AFC period. Statistics showed that merchant banks tended to outperform on their RWCR compared to commercial banks and financial companies. When we compare Tier 1 capital with Tier 2 capital, we find that the banking core capital (Tier 1) of 9.22% dropped during the AFC period, and a huge growth rate was reported for Tier 2 capital. In contrast, a change can be seen following the AFC period, with a positive growth rate of 7.19% for Tier 1 capital and a double-digit reduction (18.13%) in Tier 2 capital. Most of the risky assets held by Malaysian banks fell into the 100% weight category – for example, corporate bonds and BB-unrated bonds – with this category growing 3% during the AFC period and reducing to 8% after the crisis period. Overall, a downward trend was reported for

Table 3.1 Banking system capital strength during the AFC period

	At end of (RM millions)				Changes (%)	
	1996	*1997*	*1998*	*1999*	*1997–1998*	*1998–1999*
Tier 1 capital		46203	41941	44954.8	–9.22%	7.19%
Tier 2 capital		12584	18298	14980.8	45.41%	–18.13%
Total capital		58787	60239	59935.6	2.47%	–0.50%
Less: investment in subsidiaries and other banking institutions capital		4431	4667	5521	5.33%	18.30%
Capital base		54356	55572	54414.6	2.24%	–2.08%
Asset risk:						
0%		122174	87929	121707.4	–28.03%	38.42%
10%		31595	26160	21754.8	–17.20%	–16.84%
20%		133362	109770	103923	–17.69%	–5.33%
50%		61195	62452	67848.2	2.05%	8.64%
100%		402682	415057	381651.6	3.07%	–8.05%
Total risk-weighted assets		516995	470853	438535.8	–8.93%	–6.86%
Risk-weighted capital ratio (%)						
Banking system	10.6	10.5	11.8	12.4	12.38%	5.08%
Commercial banks	10.8	10.3	11.7	12.6	13.59%	7.69%
Financial companies	9.8	10.3	11.1	10.8	7.77%	–2.70%
Merchant banks	11.7	13.3	15.2	14.5	14.29%	–4.61%

Source: BNM Annual Report (1998, 1999)

Malaysian banks' holding of risky assets during and after the AFC period. Basel I indicated that banks maintaining their capital adequacy requirement at 8% or more could be considered stable; however, the AFC nonetheless hit Malaysian banks very badly. This suggested the importance of revisiting the Basel I capital adequacy framework, which focuses on credit and market risk only. In addition, the recapitalization assistance of Danamodal Nasional Bhd during the crisis period resulted in stable RWCR and did not indicate the true capital capability of these Malaysian banks during the AFC period.

3.1.3 Basel II: Malaysian bank policies and practices

Empirical evidence suggests that there are six aspects of risk that banks need to address – credit risk, market risk, liquidity risk, counterparty risk, legal risk, and operational risk (Santomero, 1997). The comprehensive Basel II standards were introduced in 2004 by the Basel Committee for Banking Supervision. Basel II promoted prudent and best-practice risk management of banks to increase their overall capability and competence in the current unpredictable economic climate. With a prudent and effective risk management monitoring model, banks can produce accurate risk-adjusted returns and capital considerations (BNM Annual Report, 2004). Basel II was expanded into three pillars: Pillar 1 focuses on the minimum capital requirement framework; Pillar II on the supervisory review framework; and Pillar III on market discipline (Bank International Settlement, 2004). Basel II has expanded on the Basel I minimum capital requirement framework, with the minimum capital adequacy requirement being derived from three types of risk: credit risk (standard approaches for credit risk), operational risk (basic indicator approach, standardized approach, or advanced measurement approach), and market risk. The revised measures are more risk-sensitive than those in Basel I, being more concentrated on credit risk, and from 2006 on market risk. Based on the risk-weighted capital ratio in Table 3.1, we can see how the old Basel I capital adequacy measurement (RWCR) was unable to accurately portray the risky asset exposure of Malaysian banks during the AFC period. However, the Basel Committee introduced new minimum capital adequacy requirements that presented a more holistic approach to measuring the banks' risky asset exposure.

To cater for accurate credit risk assessment in Pillar I, BNM has encouraged banks to use more integrated data and systems to identify customers for each borrower and avoid data redundancy or inconsistency. This will lead to better data quality in risk assessment across borrowers at any timeframe. The system thus facilitates banks to produce more accurate risk profiles than during the Basel I period. In 2006, BNM introduced guidelines on data quality management and management information systems (BNM Annual Report, 2006). In 2008, there was full implementation of the standard approaches to credit risk at Malaysian banks (BNM Annual Report, 2008).

Regarding the operational risk aspect, Basel II offers the basic indicator approach, the standardized approach, and the advanced measurement approach for adoption by banks in managing their operational and financial risks. A Malaysian Treasury Risk Management Section (TRMS) was introduced in 2006 to act as an independent committee for assessing banks' financial risk from their treasury activities (BNM Annual Report, 2006). The Risk Management Unit (RMU) and the Risk Management Committee (RMC) were then introduced to support best practice in Basel II risk management in Malaysia as part of an Enterprise Risk Management System. Each bank in Malaysia is required to have an in-house RMU responsible for assessing three levels of risk assessment techniques, including i) self-assessment by each department, ii) independent assessment by the RMU of each department, and iii) overall or bank-wide risk assessment by the RMC. The RMC is headed by the BNM's governor and assisted by the Operation Management Committee (ORMC) and the Financial Risk Management Committee (FRMC) (BNM Annual Report, 2010). For the bank operational risk in Pillar I, the basic indicator, the standardized approach, and the advanced measurement approach were implemented in mid-2007 (BNM Annual Report, 2007).

To deal with market risk, the Market Risk-Capital Adequacy Framework (MRCAF) was implemented among Malaysian banks in September 2005. This detailed capital regulations for addressing potential losses that banks may be exposed to through market risk (BNM Annual Report, 2004). The MRCAF was adopted from a suggestion of BIS to incorporate market risk into the capital adequacy measurement. After the AFC period, Malaysian banks have been more engaged in financial innovation products and services for risk management. Hence, with the implementation of MRCAF, banks are able to assess the level of credit risk accurately by incorporating market-wide risk factors (BNM Annual Report, 2005).

In Pillar II, Basel II emphasized an intense and close supervisory review function by central banks to ensure the effective implementation of holistic risk management and capital adequacy strategies by banks. The Pillar II comprehensive risk management system covers five processes, including a senior management monitoring mechanism, sound capital assessment, robust risk assessment techniques, monitoring and reporting, and internal risk control mechanisms. Under the second pillar, a more comprehensive risk monitoring process need to be identified and implemented by banks. Within this risk monitoring process, central banks need to ensure that the banks improve their risk management practices to overcome issues identified by the risk monitoring process flow. In response to new regulations in Basel II, BNM has extracted four basic strategies (BNM Annual Report, 2004):

i) Continue to enhance the risk management standards that need to be implemented by all banks in Malaysia. This strategy is essential if BNM is to revise and revisit its existing risk management standards according to new standards outlined by the Basel Committee from time to time.
ii) The flexibility of the timeframe for adopting the new standards derives from Basel II. Foreign banks in Malaysia tend to be more efficient than local banks in adopting new regulations imposed by Basel II; a different timeframe is therefore crucial so that local banks can internally prepare themselves to implement the new advanced approaches derived from the Basel II standards.
iii) BNM's attempts to have the Basel II provisions adopted in advance by banks was not part of the regulatory mandate, but was aimed to enhance the business justification.

iv) A more advanced and effective risk management model was introduced, which can be used by Malaysian banks in tandem with the Basel II requirements.

Like conventional banks in Malaysia, Malaysian Islamic banks also need to assess their level of capital adequacy and submit to continuous monitoring by BNM. A modified version of the capital adequacy framework, the Capital Adequacy Framework for Islamic Banking Institutions (CAFIB) was introduced in 2015, covering similar goals to those of the general capital adequacy framework; however, different Islamic risky asset classifications (Shariah contracts) are identified in computing the RWCR for Islamic banks. Islamic banks are also adopting similar approaches to those employed by conventional banks to assess their credit, operational, and market risk.

The implementation of Pillar III acts as a complementary strategy supporting the regulations from Pillar I and II. Pillar III highlights the importance of banks' disclosure of information on credit risk and operational risk measurements to stakeholders. The third Pillar focuses on overall market discipline in sharing risk information and promoted transparency regarding the disclosure of financial information to the public. In 2009, the market discipline disclosure regulations were fully implemented by Malaysian banks (BNM Annual Report, 2009).

The 2007 US mortgage subprime crisis, with its spillover to European banks, showed that a situation where banks are "too big to fail" is no longer acceptable. Table 3.2 shows that Malaysian banks were slightly affected by the GFC shocks, which radiated from the US and Europe. Malaysian banks' RWCR and CCR showed downward trends during the GFC period (2007 and 2008), but the banks were able to maintain both ratios above the minimum requirements outlined by the Basel II standards. In the profitability

Table 3.2 Key financial soundness indicators for Malaysian banks

	2005 (%)	*2006 (%)*	*2007 (%)*	*2008 (%)*	*2009 (%)**
Risk-weighted capital ratio (RWCR)	13.7	13.5	13.2	12.6	14.7
Core capital ratio (CCR)	10.7	10.7	10.2	10.6	13.1
Return on assets (ROA)	1.4	1.3	1.5	1.5	1.2
Return on equity (ROE)	16.8	16.2	19.8	18.6	13.9
Liquid assets to total assets (LtoA)	8	8	9.3	10.3	11.5
Liquid assets to short-term liabilities (LtoSTL)	10.2	10.3	11.8	13.1	14.5
Three-month NPL ratio	5.8	4.8	3.2	2.2	1.8

Source: BNM Annual Report (2009)

perspective, both return on assets (ROA) and return on equity (ROE) registered upward trends from 2005 to 2008. In contrast, the pattern after 2008 showed a ROE large drop from 18.6% to 13.9%. In addition, Malaysian banks demonstrated strong and stable liquidity positions before and after the GFC period (LtoA and LtoSTL). The effectiveness of Basel II requirements promoting high-standard credit risk monitoring translated into better performance of Malaysian banks' NPL ratios during the GFC period, compared to Malaysian banks' worst ever NPL performances during the AFC period.

Liquidity risk is another crucial aspect for banks to overcome in during the current turbulence. Liquidity risk occurs when banks are unable to meet the level of operational cash flow; this can occur under any economic climate, but is especially common in unstable periods. To ensure that the banks' liquidity risk is at a very minimal level, a range of measures, consistent monitoring, and effective regulation need to be implemented by central banks. If banks' liquidity risk is uncontrollable, bank fragility and further collapse may result. If the banking sector collapses, the market will lose confidence in the credibility of these banks to serve the market as financial intermediaries. After the AFC, this fear triggered BNM to introduce the Malaysian liquidity framework in 1998 (Bank Negara Malaysia, 2008); it provides a structured measurement for assessing bank liquidity risk in Malaysia. Based on this framework, banks are required to assess their liquidity mismatch position by forecasting their one-year assets, liabilities, and off-balance-sheet exposure maturity profile. Based on this, they need to ensure adequate liquidity cushions in both stable and unstable periods. After the GFC period, BNM revised the liquidity framework by imposing a liquidity stress-test requirement on Malaysian banks to measure the banks' liquidity in normal and abnormal market conditions. The Malaysian banking sector is relatively large globally, so to ensure that the level of liquidity risk is minimized, BNM also introduced the Liquidity Management Framework for Islamic banks in 2011 (Financial Stability and Payment Systems Report, 2011).

BNM also established a comprehensive stress-test approach to encompass macro level and micro level prudential measures in (Financial Stability and Payment Systems Report, 2012). The aim of the stress-testing procedure is to allow precautionary measures to be taken in assessing the survivability of banks in the event of a crisis. According to the Bank's financial stability framework, such testing may be top-down or bottom-up. A top-down stress-test requires banks to identify macro level scenarios and evaluate their effects on the banks' portfolio exposure. A bottom-up stress-test requires banks to gauge the response of their portfolios, on the basis of previous experiences, and to incorporate the volatility of their performances in varying market conditions. The full concept of the stress-test procedures using multiple and integrated applications is presented in Figure 3.1.

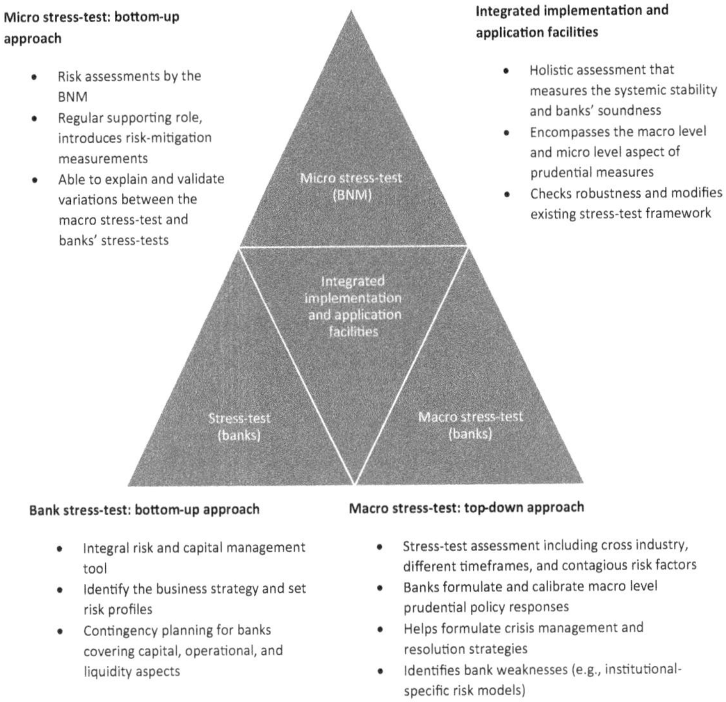

Figure 3.1 Approaches and applications of stress-testing in Malaysia

Source: Financial Stability and Payment systems Report 2012, p. 54

3.1.4 Basel III: Malaysian bank policies and practices

Since the GFC, BIS has revisited Basel II, introducing the Basel III capital requirements in 2013. Basel III is essential for further strengthening the risk-capital adequacy framework by putting emphasis on bank stability through more stable risk-weighted asset exposure by the banks in all economic climates. Basel II imposed a more comprehensive RWCR measurement, but US and European banks nonetheless collapsed during the GFC.

The Basel III RWCR modification considers three aspects, including:

i) Robustness testing and implementation of sensitivity analysis of banks' operational and credit risk.
ii) Force banks not to use internal measurement models.
iii) Enhance the existing (Basel II) RWCR by introducing a leverage ratio and revisiting the capital floor.

In Malaysia, BNM announced two phases of implementation of the Basel III standards, starting in 2015. The year 2016 was the transmission year for all banks in Malaysia to comply with the first-phase revised standard. Among the major updates in Basel III are changes related to capital requirements, leverage ratios, and liquidity ratios (LR) – the net stable funding ratio (NSFR) and the liquidity coverage ratio (LCR). BNM requires Malaysian banks to increase their LCR to 80%, starting with 2017; however LCR reporting by banks began in 2016. The consistency of the liquidity risk measurements is important in order for Malaysian banks to rely on LCR as a liquidity risk exposure, and to more easily make comparisons between banks. The NSFR requirement is more complex than the LCR requirement, as the NSFR requires banks to have stable, long-term planning to rebalance the source of funding on their assets. Based on the Financial Stability and Payments System Report (2016), a majority of Malaysian banks were reported to have over 100% in both LCR and NSFR indicators. This suggests that, overall, Malaysian banks have stable liquidity performance. However, close monitoring of the function by BNM is vital, as the central bank is targeting scores of 100% for both liquidity indicators of all banks. The second phase of the Basel III standards took effect in in 2017 and is described in Figure 3.2. The evolution of risk management regulations and domestic bank practices are summarized in Figure 3.3.

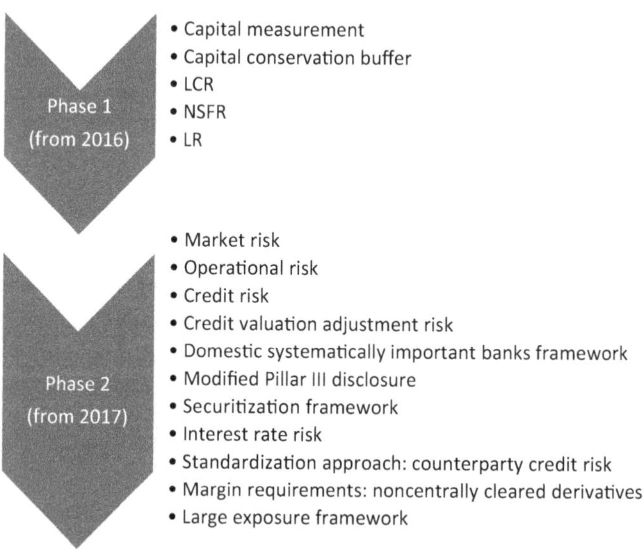

Figure 3.2 Implementation of Basel III standards in Malaysia

Reproduced from: BNM Financial Stability and Payment System Report (2016)

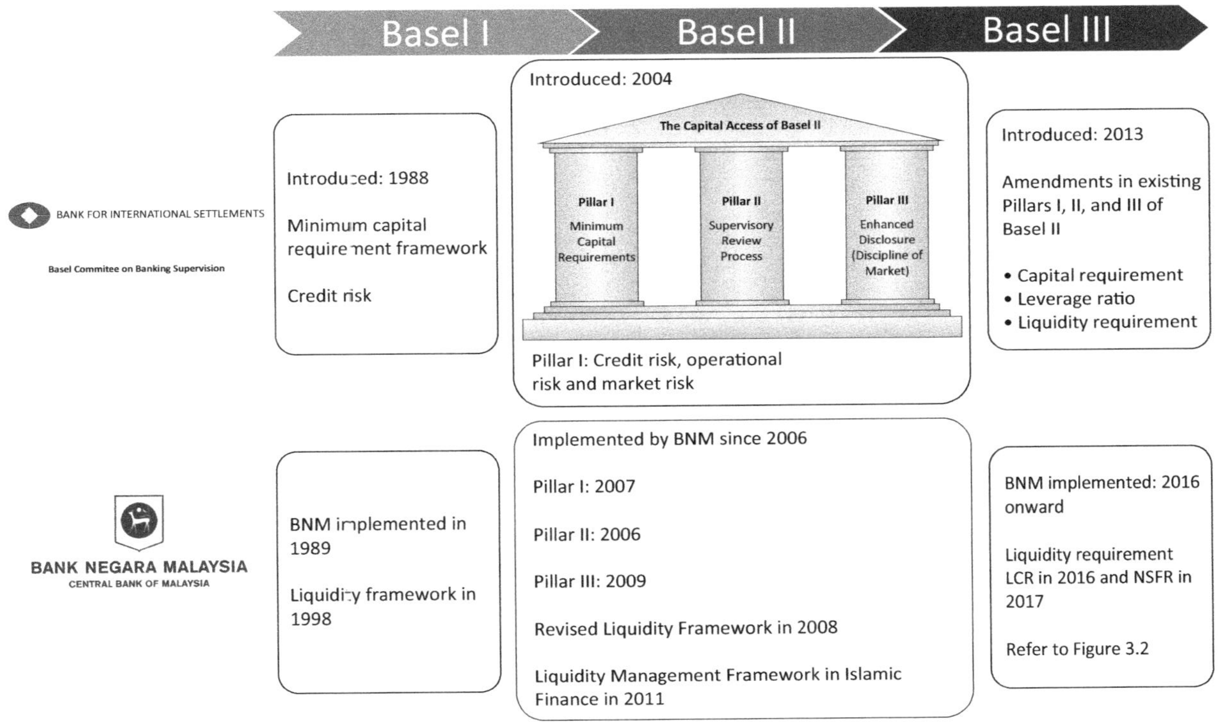

Figure 3.3 Evolution of risk management in Malaysia

3.2 Global bank best practices

The risk management practice of the banks is rather abstract, and largely depends on the objectives of the bank itself. However, there is always the regulatory interest in benchmarking and modelling the financial soundness of banks with different measures. As discussed in Section 3.1, the Basel Committee came out with various measures and policies to safeguard banks and monitor the banking system. This is crucial because disturbances in the banking system lead to impediments in the payment system, affecting the economy as a whole. This was demonstrated by two major financial crises – namely, the 1997 Asian financial crisis and the 2008 global financial crisis. The question of whether banks will be able to survive future crises is always of interest to both policy makers and academia.

Prior to the 2008 global financial crisis, we have seen that the world's largest banks (in terms of total assets) were from developed economies, such as Europe and the US (see Table 3.3). A decade later, global banks are now dominated by institutions from China (Table 3.4). From Table 3.3, we can observe that the top four banks in the world are now Chinese state-owned banks. Royal Bank of Scotland used to be the world's largest bank by asset size, but experienced a 72.94% fall in total asset value from USD $3.77 trillion to USD $1.02 trillion, ranking it 25th in 2017. The main reason behind the fall of banks in Europe and the US is the sales of US mortgages and issues in risk management.

On the other hand, the Industrial & Commercial Bank of China became the largest bank in the world in 2012, and has since maintained its status as the world's largest bank in terms of total assets. The top four banks are now

Table 3.3 Top ten banks by assets in 2007

Ranking	*Bank*	*Country*	*Total assets (USD trillion)*
1	Royal Bank of Scotland	UK	3.77
2	Deutsche Bank	Germany	2.95
3	BNP Paribas	France	2.47
4	UBS	Switzerland	2.53
5	Barclays	UK	2.43
6	HSBC	UK	2.35
7	Citigroup	US	2.19
8	Crédit Agricole	France	2.06
9	Bank of America	US	1.72
10	Société Générale	France	1.57

Source: Annual reports, S&P Global

Table 3.4 Top ten banks by assets in 2017

Ranking	*Bank*	*Country*	*Total assets (USD trillion)*
1	Industrial & Commercial Bank of China	China	3.76
2	China Construction Bank	China	3.20
3	Agricultural Bank of China	China	3.04
4	Bank of China	China	2.87
5	Mitsubishi UFJ Financial Group	Japan	2.71
6	JPMorgan Chase & Co	US	2.56
7	HSBC	UK	2.49
8	BNP Paribas	France	2.45
9	Bank of America	US	2.25
10	China Development Bank	China	2.08

Source: www.relbanks.com/worlds-top-banks/assets

all Chinese state-owned banks, which presents a paradox, as such state-owned enterprises' performance tends to be questionable, given preferential loans and manipulation by local authorities.

In this section, we examine the financial soundness of the banking system and the financial institutions involved, in order to present some insights in the rise and fall of banks in developed economies – namely the US, the UK, and China. Financial soundness indicators (FSIs) were endorsed by the International Monetary Fund's Executive Board in June 2001 to provide insight into the financial health and soundness of countries; their full implementation was in 2000. They were then reviewed in June 2003 and implemented in the mid-2000s. These FSIs provide measurements of the economic and financial stability performance for all banks in countries worldwide. Using these indicators, we proceed with this analysis to evaluate the financial soundness of the countries involved and to determine whether the FSIs provide the infrastructure for better practices at financial institutions. We use the core FSIs listed in Table 3.5 for our analysis throughout this section.

The indicators in Table 3.5 comprehensively cover financial institutions' positions under five main aspects: capital adequacy, asset quality, earnings and profitability, liquidity, and the sensitivity of the financial institutions to market risk. We analyze the performance of the overall depository institutions in the US and UK – the countries that used to have the largest banks in the world – and China, which has had the largest four banks in the world since 2017. We further compare the performance of the Malaysian banking industry to gain some insight into what should be improved to make the depository institutions more competitive on the world market in this age of globalization and liberalization.

Table 3.5 Core FSI codes for deposit takers

Code	*Ratio*
I01	Regulatory capital to risk-weighted assets
I02	Regulatory Tier 1 capital to risk-weighted assets
I03	Nonperforming loans net of provisions to capital
I04	Nonperforming loans to total gross loans
I05	Sectorial distribution of loans to total loans
I06	Return on assets
I07	Return on equity
I08	Interest margin to gross income
I09	Noninterest expenses to gross income
I10	Liquid assets to total assets
I11	Liquid assets to short-term liabilities
I12	Net open position in foreign exchange to capital

Sources: www.imf.org/external/np/sta/fsi/eng/fsi.htm

3.2.1 Financial soundness of the depository institutions

3.2.1.1 Capital adequacy indicators

Table 3.6 shows the capital adequacy indicators for depository institutions in the UK, the US, China, and Malaysia. Capital adequacy is important because it ensures that banks to have sufficient buffers to absorb reasonable losses before becoming insolvent. This is critical, especially during financial crises that can result in bank runs that put depositors' funds at stake. It also helps to ensure the efficiency and stability of the financial system of the country by lowering the risk that banking institutions become insolvent. It is thus always the main concern of banking regulators to impose minimum capital adequacy requirements on financial institutions, and especially on depository institutions.

From Table 3.6, we observed that depository institutions in the UK have the highest regulatory capital to risk-weighted assets and regulatory Tier 1 capital to risk-weighted assets, with an average of 18% and 14.76%, respectively. This is followed by Malaysian depository institutions with an average of 16.50% and 13.51%, respectively. This may be due to the fact that the regulator in the UK has been trying to strengthen capital requirements of the depository institutions by implementing Basel III since the GFC. Similarly, in Malaysia, capital requirements continue to be important for the banking authority, which is attempting to safeguard banking institutions in the face of the challenge of the growing globalization in the country. Furthermore, lessons learnt during the AFC have led the Malaysian banking authority to further revise and strength capital requirements in the country.

Table 3.6 Capital adequacy indicators

	2010	*2011*	*2012*	*2013*	*2014*	*2015*	*2016*	*Mean*
				UK				
Regulatory capital to risk-weighted assets	15.89	15.73	17.07	19.61	17.31	19.62	20.8	18.00
Regulatory Tier 1 capital to risk-weighted assets	13.23	13.31	14.51	16.08	13.63	15.69	16.88	14.76
Nonperforming loans net of provisions to capital	16.86	16.11	13.87	9.48	5.38	3.88	3.45	9.86
				US				
Regulatory capital to risk-weighted assets	14.79	14.69	14.51	14.41	14.39	14.14	14.19	14.45
Regulatory Tier 1 capital to risk-weighted assets	12.46	12.63	12.7	12.8	13.09	13.09	13.17	12.85
Nonperforming loans net of provisions to capital	20	17.59	15.66	11.7	8.83	7.23	6.62	12.52
				China				
Regulatory capital to risk-weighted assets	12.16	12.71	13.25	12.19	13.18	13.45	13.28	12.89
Regulatory Tier 1 capital to risk-weighted assets	10.08	10.24	10.62	9.95	10.76	11.31	11.25	10.60
Nonperforming loans net of provisions to capital	–2.14	–4	–4.46	–11.62	–9.79	–7.87	–7.81	–6.81
				Malaysia				
Regulatory capital to risk-weighted assets	17.45	17.7	17.64	14.58	15.36	16.28	16.48	16.50
Regulatory Tier 1 capital to risk-weighted assets	13.52	13.15	13.41	13.12	13.43	13.95	14.02	13.51
Nonperforming loans net of provisions to capital	13.93	11.57	8.34	8.06	7.04	6.78	6.67	8.91

Source: Financial Soundness Indicators, International Monetary Fund

China remains behind the developed countries and Malaysia in terms of regulatory capital requirements. We nevertheless observed that Chinese depository institutions are far superior to the depository institutions in other countries in terms of nonperforming loans net provisions to capital, with a reported average of -6.81%. This is rather impressive, as the banking industry in China is dominated by state-owned banks, which are often criticized

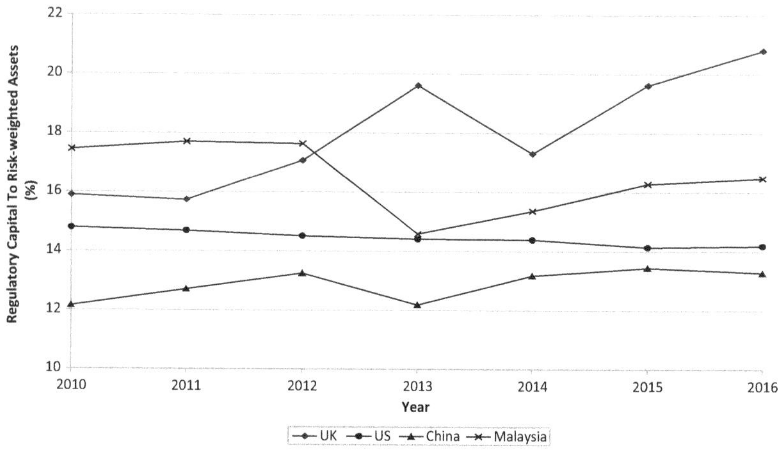

Figure 3.4 Regulatory capital to risk-weighted assets

for their high level of nonperforming loans. We take a closer look at the components of capital adequacy in each country in our analysis. Figure 3.4 shows the trends in regulatory capital to risk-weighted assets for each country of interest.

From Figure 3.4, we see that depository institutions in the UK steadily improved their regulatory capital to risk-weighted assets after the GFC, reaching as high as 20.8% in 2016 despite a decrease in the regulatory capital to risk-weighted assets and the regulatory Tier 1 capital to risk-weighted assets (refer to Figure 3.5) in 2014. On the other hand, depository institutions in the US still experienced reductions in capital adequacy until 2013, and this shows how severely the GFC affected banking institutions in the US. Nevertheless, implementation of the Basel III and Capital Purchase Program in that country slowly helped to recapitalize US banking institutions, with a steady growth in regulatory Tier 1 capital to risk-weighted assets since 2013. We also note that the regulatory capital to risk-weighted assets ratio is still decreasing.

Overall, in context of capital adequacy, UK and Malaysian banks tend to have stronger capital positions than US and Chinese banks. In addition, the Chinese banks registered outstanding performance with lower nonperforming loan positions.

We observe that since 2010, depository institutions in China are slowly picking up in terms of regulatory capital to risk-weighted assets and regulatory Tier 1 capital to risk-weighted assets. This may due to the fact that the government further enhanced risk management practices at depository institutions with the introduction of a corporate law. This may also have

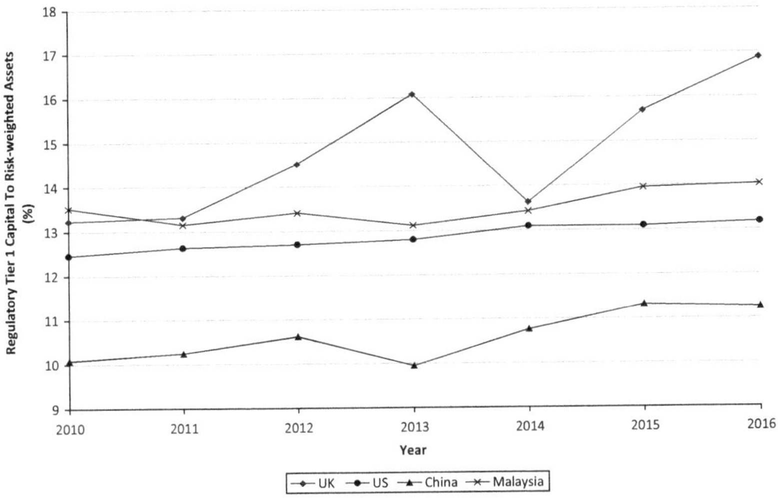

Figure 3.5 Regulatory Tier 1 capital to risk-weighted assets

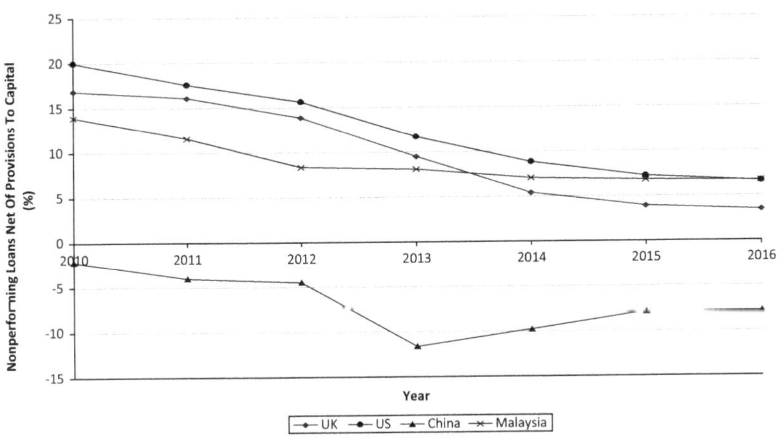

Figure 3.6 Nonperforming loans net of provisions to capital

led to the lower nonperforming loans net of provisions to capital than other countries (Figure 3.6). Even though the Chinese nonperforming loans net of provisions to capital is lower than that of other countries in our analysis, we observe that the nonperforming loans net of provisions to capital began to pick up in 2013. This could serve as a sign of market disruption if not handled carefully. Such an increase in nonperforming loans net of provisions to capital may due to volatility in the stock market in recent years, which significantly increased the nonperforming loans of the depository institutions in the country.

From Figure 3.6, the nonperforming loans net of provisions to capital for all the countries are decreasing, which indicates an improvement in financial soundness in the UK, US, and Malaysia as well.

3.2.1.2 Asset quality indicators

The second aspect of financial stability and soundness indicators is asset quality perspective. All banks are required to declare their asset quality to central banks and the public, so these ratios are among the most important indicators for gauging banks' stability positions. The overall asset quality is primarily dependent on the quality of the loan portfolio and credit administration program, since loans typically constitute the major portfolio for depository institutions. The two core ratios stressed by the FSIs for deposit takers are i) nonperforming loans to total gross loans and ii) sectorial distribution of loans to total loans.

In Table 3.7, the nonperforming loans to total gross loans ratio is an important indicator for banks, as a high nonperforming loans ratio will expose banks to high solvency risk positions, meaning risk of a situation where a bank is unable to collect loan repayments from defaulting customers; this thus affects the bank's earnings, as lending is its main financial services activity. It will also increase the bank's operating costs for managing nonperforming loans. We observe that the nonperforming loans to total gross loans in the US was highest, with a reported average of 2.65%; this was followed by the UK, with an average of nonperforming loans to total gross loans of 2.60% from 2010 to 2016. Although the US and UK have the highest average of nonperforming loans to total gross loans, the ratio has been steadily decreasing over the years, as a result of the action taken by banking authorities to improve the overall health of depository institutions after the GFC.

Similarly, we also observed that the ratio of nonperforming loans to total gross loans in China was lowest, remaining between 0.95% and 1.74%. Nevertheless, depository institutions in China have begun to experience an increase in the nonperforming loans to total gross loans since 2013, and this outcome is consistent with the ratio of nonperforming loans net of provisions to capital. Even though Chinese depository institutions have performed well since the GFC, we should not disregard the increase in nonperforming loans lightly, as it may result in inefficiency and an increase in operating costs.

Next the sectorial distribution of loans to total loans shows the concentration of loans, and hence indicates the diversification of loans in terms of risk management. Table 3.7 shows that the UK and China have the largest

Table 3.7 Asset quality indicators

	2010	*2011*	*2012*	*2013*	*2014*	*2015*	*2016*	*Mean*
				UK				
Nonperforming loans to total gross loans	3.95	3.96	3.59	3.11	1.65	1.01	0.94	2.60
Sectorial distribution of loans to total loans	13.21	14.37	14.85	16.33	11.52	11.20	10.05	***13.08***
				US				
Nonperforming loans to total gross loans	4.39	3.78	3.32	2.45	1.85	1.47	1.32	***2.65***
Sectorial distribution of loans to total loans	6.02	5.98	6.01	4.97	4.08	3.59	3.81	4.92
				China				
Nonperforming loans to total gross loans	1.13	0.96	0.95	1.00	1.25	1.67	1.74	1.24
Sectorial distribution of loans to total loans	9.56	9.9	11.38	11.19	8.76	7.07	3.72	8.80
				Malaysia				
Nonperforming loans to total gross loans	3.35	2.68	2.02	1.85	1.65	1.60	1.61	2.11
Sectorial distribution of loans to total loans	0.01	0.05	0.04	0.06	0.03	0.05	0.05	0.04

Source: Financial Soundness Indicators, International Monetary Fund

loan concentrations, with an average of 13.08% and 8.80%, respectively. The high loan concentration in the UK might be due to the fact that most of the loans are residential loans, whereas in China most loans are made to the priority sectors, as the country is dominated by state-owned banks. We noticed that the concentration decreased over time in all the countries, which implies that regulators are now paying more attention to diversify their sectorial loan concentration in order to avoid repeating the history of the GFC.

On the basis of the asset quality indicators, Chinese banks were able to maintain a low nonperforming loan value, with Malaysian banks having the second lowest NPL position of the four countries considered. The evidence indicates that Chinese and Malaysian banks are in a better position to maintain their NPL performances. This may be due to strict prudential measures implemented by the central banks of these countries. From the perspective of loan diversification, UK and Chinese banks tend to be more diversified in giving out loans, while Malaysian banks need to enhance their loan diversification and not concentrate in certain industries. Such low diversification may expose the bank to unsystematic risk.

3.2.1.3 Earning and profitability indicators

The core earnings and profitability indicators emphasized by the FSIs for depository institutions are presented in Table 3.8. It is clear that Chinese depository institutions emerge as most profitable, being superior in terms of

Table 3.8 Earnings and profitability indicators

	2010	*2011*	*2012*	*2013*	*2014*	*2015*	*2016*	*Mean*
				UK				
Return on assets	0.32	0.29	0.17	0.22	0.33	0.28	0.25	0.27
Return on equity	6.87	6.11	3.24	3.83	5.58	4.42	3.77	4.83
Interest margin to gross income	50.43	44.19	49.35	50.92	48.42	50.99	46.19	48.64
Noninterest expenses to gross income	69.08	61.08	76.14	81.04	64.11	71.12	76.31	71.27
				US				
Return on assets	0.23	0.28	0.33	0.38	0.33	0.36	0.37	0.33
Return on equity	1.81	2.25	2.72	3.26	2.82	3.03	3.16	2.72
Interest margin to gross income	63.55	65.18	60.83	63.49	63.73	63.40	65.09	63.61
Noninterest expenses to gross income	62.47	64.51	63.56	61.71	64.66	60.69	59.55	62.45
				China				
Return on assets	1.13	1.28	1.28	1.27	1.23	1.10	0.98	1.18
Return on equity	19.22	20.40	19.85	19.17	17.59	14.98	13.38	17.80
Interest margin to gross income	82.53	80.68	80.17	78.85	78.53	76.27	76.20	79.03
Noninterest expenses to gross income	35.31	33.37	33.10	32.90	31.62	30.59	31.11	32.57
				Malaysia				
Return on assets	1.54	1.51	1.58	1.49	1.49	1.24	1.35	1.46
Return on equity	16.28	16.8	17.31	15.77	15	12.26	12.31	15.10
Interest margin to gross income	59.82	53.48	54.78	59.6	61	61.82	61.04	58.79
Noninterest expenses to gross income	41.52	45.25	45.02	42.57	42.97	46.67	43.99	44.00

Source: Financial Soundness Indicators, International Monetary Fund

return on equity and interest margin to gross income. This demonstrates that depository institutions in China are not only fundamentally strong in terms of asset quality, as mentioned previously, but also superior in their earning ability. These factors enabled Chinese banks to become the largest banks in the world in 2012. Furthermore, compared to depository institutions in the other countries, Chinese institutions managed their expenses more efficiently with low noninterest expenses to gross income fluctuating over the years between 31.11% and 35.31%.

We noticed that depository institutions in the UK and the US experienced low earnings ratios as well as high noninterest expenses to gross income. This may due to the expenses incurred by the institutions in managing and reconsolidating their resources after the GFC. In this context, the expenses for depository institutions in the UK are the highest, with an average of 71.27% since 2010. This needs to be taken care of in order not to put the depository institutions at risk and to continue to be able to withstand future adverse economic events. Surprisingly, Malaysian banks were able to generate higher return on each of their assets investment than the banks of the developed countries.

3.2.1.4 Liquidity indicators

A bank's liquidity position safeguards it from a shortage of cash during a bank run and from losses in value during adverse economic events. We witnessed the run on US banks, which led to a liquidity risk during the GFC, resulting in bank failures in developed economies. Similarly, banks failed in the Asian economies during the AFC. The liquidity ratios are presented in Table 3.9 in terms of assets and short-terms liabilities.

From Table 3.9, we can see that the liquid assets to total assets ratio of depository institutions in China is the highest, with an average of 13.15%. In fact, the institutions maintain a strong position in the liquid assets to total assets, which is always above 20%. This indicates the ability of the depository institutions to cover their obligations with liquid assets in the case of sudden withdrawal. The depository institutions in the UK also maintain high liquid assets to total assets ratio, with an average of 21%. However, the liquid asset ratio has decreased since 2013, which may lead to banks ending up in an unfavourable position should the decrease continue.

The next liquidity indicator is liquid assets to short-term liabilities, which shows the maturity mismatch in the depository institutions and also the extent to which banks could meet short-term withdrawals of funds without facing liquidity problems. Higher ratios may mean that banks are able to meet the short-term withdrawal, but also means that too many assets are

Table 3.9 Liquidity indicators

	2010	*2011*	*2012*	*2013*	*2014*	*2015*	*2016*	*Mean*
UK								
Liquid assets to total assets	20.96	20.47	22.51	22.70	21.25	19.51	19.63	21.00
Liquid assets to short-term liabilities	37.90	40.89	36.81	35.69	35.69	35.89	37.92	37.26
US								
Liquid assets to total assets	10.83	12.69	13.42	14.53	14.54	13.20	12.82	13.15
Liquid assets to short-term liabilities	47.28	66.11	74.11	88.35	90.03	91.20	98.20	***79.33***
China								
Liquid assets to total assets	22.61	21.21	21.10	21.23	19.89	21.12	21.35	***21.22***
Liquid assets to short-term liabilities	42.20	43.16	45.83	44.03	46.44	48.01	47.55	45.32
Malaysia								
Liquid assets to total assets	15.71	12.93	13.82	13.16	13.33	22.11	21.22	16.10
Liquid assets to short-term liabilities	48.13	36.58	42.53	40.95	43.18	141.77	134.46	73.25

Source: Financial Soundness Indicators, International Monetary Fund

held in short-term forms, which banks may need to be cognizant of when considering earnings. We note that depository institutions in the US and Malaysia generally kept their assets in short-term forms, with averages of 79.33% and 73.25%, respectively. It is worth noticing that the depository institutions have held too much liquidity in the recent years, with the ratio reaching as high as 141.77% in 2015 and 134.46% in 2016. This may result in banks compromising on their earnings, as too many assets are locked in short-term assets, generating smaller profits. On the other hand, Chinese institutions show well-balanced funds in terms of their short-term assets and short-term liabilities. This may also have contributed to the higher earnings ability of the depository institutions in China (Table 3.9).

3.2.1.5 Bank sensitivity toward market risk indicators

Finally, the net open position in foreign exchange to capital measures the sensitivity of banking institutions to market risk. This ratio is summarized in Table 3.10. We note that depository institutions in the UK exhibit the highest exposure to market risk, at an average of 116.69% mainly due to

Table 3.10 Net open position in foreign exchange to capital

	2010	*2011*	*2012*	*2013*	*2014*	*2015*	*2016*	*Mean*
UK	82.07	157.96	123.39	120.77	73.60	133.80	125.25	116.69
US	NA	NA	NA	NA	NA	NA	NA	NA
China	6.73	4.58	3.92	3.68	3.50	3.67	3.54	***4.23***
Malaysia	9.31	14.65	14.07	13.76	13.2	12.46	13.07	12.93

Source: Financial Soundness Indicators, International Monetary Fund

increase in exposure in 2015 and 2016. This served as a market signal of the riskiness of these depository institutions. On the other hand, the sensitivity of Chinese banks to market risk reduced over time, with a reported average of 4.23%. A unique upward trend is seen in Malaysian banks' foreign exposure toward capital from 2010 to 2012. In 2012, BNM imposed a new requirement – macro stress-tests via a top-down approach for each bank; this is a self-assessment evaluating Malaysian banks' macro level sensitivity towards their major performances, including cross-industry, different time-frames, and contagious risk factors. The macro stress-test gives the bank an insight into how stable it is and how ready it is to absorb any external turbulence. A downward trend can be seen for Malaysian banks' foreign exchange exposure since 2013. This might be due to internal bank measures to overcome the volatility of banks' foreign currency borrowing obligation given the depreciation of the Malaysian ringgit against the US dollar.

In summary, based on these five types of indicators, we can deduce that the rise of depository institutions in China may due to their ability to generate higher earnings and profitability than banks in the other countries, controlling their asset quality while reducing the sensitivity of their position to market risk. Malaysian banks are better off than US banks in term of capital adequacy, asset quality, and liquidity. However, Malaysian banks need to further diversify their loan concentration distributions. We next compare the performance of the individual top banks in the UK, US, China, and Malaysia to gain some insight into their rise and fall over recent years.

3.2.2 Performance of individual banks

In this subsection, we look at lending banks in the UK, US, China, and Malaysia, comparing their performance in order to gain some insight into the rise and fall of the world's leading banks. We focus on the profitability and risk of the banks. We first look at the performance of Royal Bank of Scotland, the world's largest bank by total assets in 2007.

As indicated by Table 3.11, Royal Bank of Scotland's profitability was greatly affected by the GFC; since 2007, the bank has experienced negative

Table 3.11 Royal Bank of Scotland's performance

Indicator	*Industry median*	*2007*	*2008*	*2009*	*2010*	*2011*	*2012*	*2013*	*2014*	*2015*	*2016*
Profitability											
Net interest margin	1.92%	2.27	1.99	1.74	2.01	1.92	1.92	2.01	2.13	2.12	2.18
Efficiency ratio*	75.20%	63.80	178.80	68.60	68.40	71.50	100.00	104.00	92.00	123.40	126.00
Operating leverage	0.90%	–1.30	–128.40	95.30	0.20	–4.00	–33.60	–3.40	10.20	–31.00	–2.00
Pretax return on assets	0.60%	0.70	–1.20	–0.10	0.00	–0.10	–0.40	–0.80	0.30	–0.30	–0.50
Pretax return on equity	9.20%	21.10	–45.90	–3.90	–0.20	–1.90	–7.30	–13.90	4.60	–5.00	–8.00
Risk											
Loan loss provision (percent of average loans)	0.22%	1.30	1.41	1.83	1.55	1.82	1.19	1.98	–0.37	–0.23	0.15
Tier 1 risk-adjusted capital ratio	15.70%	7.30	10.00	14.10	12.90	13.00	12.40	13.10	–	16.30	15.20

* Efficiency ratio presents the cost to income ratio which indicates the efficiency of the banks in managing their expenses given the income generated. Higher efficiency ratio in this case indicates higher expenses incurred by the banks in managing the banks and hence banks are considered as inefficient in their cost management.

Source: Thomson Reuters Eikon

returns in assets and equity. This may be due to lending losses that led to a reduction in profit of more than 400% from 2007 to 2008. This shifted the bank's ranking from the largest bank in the world in terms of total assets to its current 25th position. This bank was also below the industry average for earning ability, as reported by Table 3.11. The Tier 1 risk-adjusted capital ratio improved over time but is still below the industry median. This explains why the ranking of the bank has dropped over the years. Furthermore, the bank is inefficient, having had an efficiency ratio of above 100% since 2015. This means that the bank is incurring a high percentage of non-interest expense to income over the recent years due to its inefficiency in managing its resources.

The performance indicators for Citigroup, the largest bank in the US, are presented in Table 3.12. The performance of Citigroup was affected during the GFC period. In 2008, its profitability dropped by 2.50% in terms of return on assets and 41.10% in terms of return on equity. As compared to Royal Bank of Scotland, Citigroup is better in terms of return on assets and return on equity, as we observed that the ratios have improved since 2010. This may indicate the effectiveness of the Capital Purchase Program, which was implemented in 2009. Furthermore, we observed that the efficiency ratio of Citigroup improved since 2014, though it has remained below the industry median of 65.90% since 2015. This shows the commitment of the bank in improving its performance as part of the Capital Purchase Program. The Tier 1 risk-adjusted capital ratio improved over time and has been above the industry median since 2010.

Table 3.13 shows the performance indicators of the world's largest bank in 2017 – the Industrial and Commercial Bank of China. The performance indicators clearly show that this bank is far superior to both Royal Bank of Scotland and Citigroup, having steadily improved in terms of return, and especially in terms of return on equity. This shows the efficiency of the bank in generating its return using the equity capital. Further, the bank maintains low credit risk, as indicated by the loan loss provision to average loan ratio always being below 1% since 2007; it increased by only 28 percentage points during 2008, demonstrating the solvency of the bank even during the GFC.

Finally, we compare the largest bank in Malaysia – Malayan Banking Berhad (Maybank) – with the Industrial and Commercial Bank of China to see how far we are from the world's largest bank. To do this, we compare the average performance of Malayan Banking Berhad with that of Industrial and Commercial Bank of China, from 2010 to 2016 – see Table 3.14.

Table 3.14 clearly shows that the largest bank in Malaysia falls behind the world's largest bank, especially in terms of return on equity, with an average

Table 3.12 Citigroup's performance

Indicator	*Industry median*	*2007*	*2008*	*2009*	*2010*	*2011*	*2012*	*2013*	*2014*	*2015*	*2016*
Profitability											
Net interest margin	3.48%	2.42	3.13	3.05	3.12	2.82	2.82	–	2.90	2.93	2.86
Efficiency ratio	65.9%	77.40	136.20	59.50	54.60	66.30	73.60	64.30	72.10	58.20	59.60
Operating leverage	2.0%	–26.60	–50.70	86.80	8.90	–19.30	–9.80	14.00	–12.30	19.10	–2.20
Pretax return on assets	1.4%	0.00	–2.50	–0.40	0.70	0.80	0.40	1.10	0.80	1.40	1.20
Pretax return on equity	12.8%	0.60	–41.10	–5.30	8.30	8.60	4.30	10.10	7.10	11.50	9.60
Risk											
Loan loss provision (percent of average loans)	0.22%	2.35	4.72	6.55	4.44	1.85	1.68	1.19	1.07	1.15	1.11
Tier 1 risk-adjusted capital ratio	12.20%	7.12	11.92	11.67	12.91	13.55	14.06	13.37	13.07	14.81	15.29

Source: Thomson Reuters Eikon

Table 3.13 Industrial and Commercial Bank of China's performance

Indicator	*Industry median*	*2007*	*2008*	*2009*	*2010*	*2011*	*2012*	*2013*	*2014*	*2015*	*2016*
Profitability											
Net interest margin	2.63%	2.80	2.95	2.26	2.44	2.61	2.66	2.57	2.66	2.47	2.16
Efficiency ratio	62.7%	43.50	36.50	39.90	37.20	37.30	37.30	38.20	38.60	38.00	36.10
Operating leverage	0.7%	2.60	18.90	–9.40	8.30	–0.40	0.10	–2.80	–1.10	1.40	4.90
Pretax return on assets	1.6%	1.40	1.60	1.60	1.70	1.90	1.90	1.90	1.80	1.70	1.60
Pretax return on equity	16.2%	22.90	25.40	26.20	28.80	30.60	29.70	28.20	25.80	21.90	19.30
Risk											
Loan loss provision (percent of average loans)	1.22%	0.95	1.28	0.45	0.45	0.43	0.41	0.41	0.55	0.77	0.71
Tier 1 risk-adjusted capital ratio	12.79%	10.99	10.75	9.90	9.97	10.07	10.62	10.62	12.19	13.48	13.42

Source: Thomson Reuters Eikon

Table 3.14 Comparison between Malayan Banking Berhad and the Industrial and Commercial Bank of China

Indicator (%)	*Industrial and Commercial Bank of China*	*Malayan Banking Berhad*	*Difference*
	Profitability		
Net interest margin	2.56	2.52	0.04
Efficiency ratio	38.26	50.52	−12.26
Operating leverage	2.25	−5.08	7.33
Pretax return on assets	1.71	1.52	0.19
Pretax return on equity	25.88	18.84	7.04
	Risk		
Loan loss provision (percent ofaverage loans)	0.64	0.39	0.25
Tier 1 risk-adjusted capital ratio	11.20	11.91	−0.71

of 7.04% per year. Malayan Banking Berhad is also less efficient, with an efficiency ratio 12.26% higher than that of the Industrial and Commercial Bank of China. This means that Maybank needs to improve its asset allocation to avoid excessive expense and allow it to be competitive with other world banks.

3.3 Future challenges for the banking industry

Changes in regulations have improved bank operations and helped mitigate the risks faced by banking institutions. This has avoided economic payment systems being negatively affected as in past financial crises. Despite the various regulations implemented by central banks and regulatory authorities around the world, banking institutions continue to be faced with challenges that arise not only from operations, but also from various third parties – especially in the era of the emerging digital economy. The future of the banking industry may involve even more uncertainty, requiring high levels of preparedness on the part of industry participants. The complex environment of the future requires a fundamental redefinition of the relationship between banks and their customers. According to the report of KPMG (2017), there are two goals to be aimed for by banks that intend to lead the market. First, they must ensure growth in market share while increasing the margin; secondly, they need to protect their high-value segments and clients. This will provide banks with competitive advantage in the future.

3.3.1 Challenges from inside the industry

3.3.1.1 Banks and customers

The relationship between banks and customers is changing as a result of the shift towards the digital economy, hence it will induce the banks operational risk. This is driven by the introduction of new technologies that lead to changes in consumer preferences which are capable of exposing banks to new types of unforeseen risks that are not yet fully understood. This has been viewed as a disruption in the business model of banks, rather than an opportunity for the banking industry, as reported by KPMG (2017). To seize the opportunity and prepare the banking industry to face the challenges of the digital economy, banks in general need to understand the demographical cohort groups in Table 3.15 in order to further strategize their business to take full advantage of each business opportunity. On the basis CGI's study (2014) of digital transformations in the banking industry, involving banking consumers from the US, Canada, France, Germany, Sweden, and the UK, banks need to understand digital consumer behaviours, preferences, and choices. This will lead to major customer-centric changes within enterprises (CGI, 2014).

Generally, the millennials have demonstrated different buying patterns and expectations in the US (KPMG, 2017). Interestingly, other cohort groups are starting to follow expectations in the US, while in Japan and European countries these millennials have been aggressively pursued (KPMG, 2017). In respect of bank consumers, a key finding in CGI's analysis (2014) shows that almost 81% of respondents expected that they would be rewarded for loyalty and valued for their total spending on credit cards. To cater for these expectations, many banks have introduced rewards programs, loyalty cards, cash-back offers, loyalty discounts, etc. (CGI, 2014). Interestingly, a recent study of Wollan et al. (2017) reveals that 91% of financial services have a loyalty program, but only 15% of the banks' consumers are extremely satisfied with

Table 3.15 Demographic cohort groups

Demographic cohort groups	
Age	*Group*
0–16	Gen-Z
16–35	Millennials
36–51	Gen-X
52–70	Baby boomers
71–88	Silent generation
over 89	Greatest generation

this program. The future of rewards programs in the banking sector requires banks to provide programs that provide value to their consumers and are more personalized to individual preferences (McIntyre, 2017). This view has also been echoed by CGI's findings (2014) that customers seek tailored services that add value. At the heart of these is the use of application programming interfaces (APIs), through which a bank can share their customer information with retailers. As the intermediate of every financial transaction, the bank possesses a treasure trove of consumer information, including on the transactions needed to personalize rewards. A good example is the preferred payment method of the customer. The risk of a security breach through an API is almost non-existent due to data encryption, which perhaps is in line with government regulation. As highlighted by a senior analyst of Forrester research, Peter Wannemacher, banks that embrace APIs early are in a better position than their competitors (Yurcan, 2016).

3.3.1.2 Operations costs

Another challenge in the banking sector is the cost of operations, especially labour costs. As shown in Figure 3.7, salaries and benefits have increased since 2010 in line with the efficiency ratio which is within 60–75% of the aggregated efficiency ratio of the US top 15 banks.

It is essential that banks seek alternatives to labour, such as automated algorithms or robotics (KPMG, 2017). According to KPMG (2017), the cost of automated algorithms or robotics (automated process) is lower and can eliminate between three to five full-time employee equivalents. This replacement has created digital labour that has been expanded to play the role of human labour in banking industries such as call centres, credit processing, client on boarding, etc. Additionally, the banking sector is facing new types

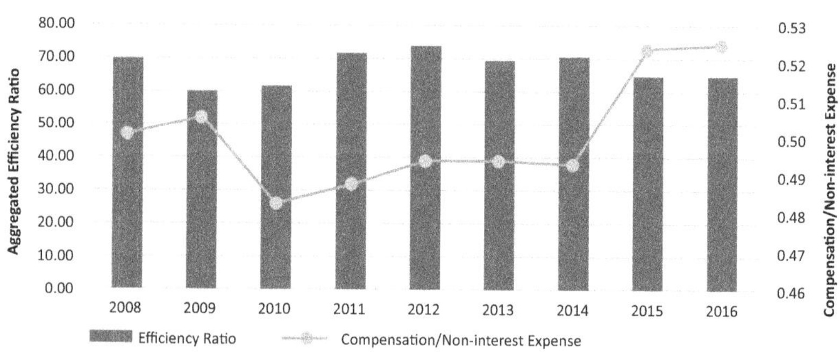

Figure 3.7 Compensation cost at the top 15 US banks

Source: KPMG (2017)

of competitors that are expected to come from even more different industries. The traditional role of the banking sector in fund transfers is now being challenged by nonbank institutions like PayPal, Western Union, Amazon Payment, Google Wallet, MoneyGram, and Venmo, and rumours are even circulating that Facebook Messenger will follow suit. The alternative services provided by these nonbank institutions give consumers more options in seeking money transfer services that are not limited to the transfer services provided by banks. There will thus be less demand for this service in banks.

3.3.2 The external threat: fintech

In an interview with CNBC, the founder of debt refinancing company Renaud Laplanche stated that there is an opportunity to make finance more cost-efficient, more friendly, and more transparent than the banking sector (Ahmed et al., 2015). This is a typical technology entrepreneur from a new sector known as financial technology, or fintech. *The Economist* has indicated that more than USD $25 billion has been invested globally from 2010 to 2015 in fintech, which is challenging banks in almost every product and service that they offer (Ong, 2016). It covers financial product administration, vetting, marketing, distribution, and supervision (Mahomed and Mohamad, 2016). The growth of fintech is tremendous – for example, from 2013 to 2015 it grew 200% year on year (Mahomed and Mohamad, 2016).

Fintech has enhanced the activity of borrowing and investing money for the individual and for businesses, while the banking sector has slacked off. This all began after the 2008 global financial crisis, when fintech companies became an alternative source of finance due to the banking sector's credit squeeze (Ahmed et al., 2015). As noted by Pollari (2016), there are six drivers behind fintech: changing consumer behaviour and preferences, digital and mobile devices, the accelerating pace of change, declining levels of trust, falling barriers to entry for digital disruptors, attractive profit pools, and support from the policy and regulatory environments.

Leading the world market, China has now overtaken London and Silicon Valley to become the centre of global fintech innovation and adoption (Jones, 2017). This was the finding of Ernst & Young and Singapore Bank DBS in November 2016, which suggested that Shanghai, Hangzhou, Beijing, and Shenzhen in particular are leading Chinese fintech. Furthermore, based on a Citigroup analysis, from January to September 2016, China accounted for more than 50% of fintech globally (Jones, 2017). China also dominates in fintech "unicorns" (start-up companies with a value of over $1 billion), with eight of the world's 27 unicorns. The world's four largest fintech companies are also Chinese: these are Ant Financial ($60 billion), Lufax ($18.5 billion), JD Finance ($7.0 billion), and Qufenqi ($5.9 billion) (Jones, 2017).

3.3.3 The Malaysian experience

In the May 2016 maiden speech of the newly appointed Governor of BNM, Muhammad Ibrahim, at the fifth Global Islamic Finance Forum, he said:

> Fintech is challenging the status quo of the financial industry. New business models will emerge. Delivery channels will challenge existing norms. Transaction costs will be reduced. Rather than looking at the fintech revolution as unwelcoming, financial in*stitutions ought to embrace it as an opportunity.*
>
> (Ibrahim, 2016)

He also highlighted in his speech that 10% to 40% of overall banking revenues could be at risk by 2025 due to fintech innovations outside banking institutions (Ibrahim, 2016). As compared to his predecessor, he was quick to react to fintech by developing a regulatory framework that will be discussed later. With a population of 31 million, Malaysia has high mobile and internet penetration, at about 141% and 81%, respectively (Omar, 2017). The biggest fintech segment is payments, at about 18% of Malaysian fintech. Blockchain, at only 4% of fintech overall, might see some interesting developments in Malaysia in the future (Pikri, 2017). It is often assumed that blockchain and Bitcoin are the same, though in fact the latter relies on blockchain technology. Blockchain is essentially a decentralized ledger that cannot be tampered with, since the data is sent to a very large network which validates the information. This is what has made Bitcoin so successful. A new player in blockchain technology, NEM.io, has entered the Malaysian market and is leveraging USD $40 million to develop a physical, nonprofit blockchain centre in Malaysia, which was scheduled to open in August 2017 (Pikri, 2017).

Broadly, the fintech sector falls under the purview of two statutory bodies in Malaysia:

i) Bank Negara Malaysia

The key role of the central bank is in promoting monetary and financial stability in Malaysia. It is governed by the Central Bank of Malaysia Act 2009. It began operation on January 26, 1959. The government of Malaysia, through BNM, has demonstrated high interest in fintech growth. Several initiatives have been put forward by the central bank, including:

- The Fintech Technology Enablement Group (FTEG), established in June 2016. FTEG describes a company as fintech if it utilizes or plans to utilize fintech but is not a financial institution. After two months of operation, FTEG unveiled a regulatory fintech sandbox which provides a 12-month testing period in which any extension request must be made in written form. No conditions are imposed on such firms in Malaysia. Already in June 2016, four sandbox participants had been approved in three categories, including financial aggregators (GoBear and GetCover), P2P currency exchange and remittance (MoneyMatch), and remittance (WorldRemit).

ii) Securities Commission of Malaysia (SC)

The Securities Commission is responsible for regulating and systematically developing Malaysia's capital market. It was established on March 1, 1993. Initiatives include:

- Alliance of Fintech Community (aFINity@SC)

  Launched in 2015 during the World Capital Markets Symposium held in Kuala Lumpur, with three purposes: i) to drive awareness and catalyze the development of fintech, ii) to create hubs to organize and nurture the fintech ecosystem, and iii) to provide policy and regulatory clarity to enhance innovation.

- Equity crowdfunding platform (ECF)

  The ECF was established in 2015, with Malaysia being the first Asia Pacific country to legislate for equity crowdfunding platforms. Within 12 months, issuers can raise up to RM 3 million, but not exceeding RM 5 million. All operators must be locally incorporated. The six current operators are FundedByMe, CrowdPlus.asia, Eureeca, Crowdo, Ata Plus, and pitchIN Equity.

- Peer-to-peer financing

  Malaysia was the first ASEAN country to regulate P2P financing in 2016. The requirement is that all P2P platforms are locally incorporated with a minimum paid-up capital of RM 5 million. Such platforms are mainly intended for private companies rather than for individuals. Currently, six operators have been granted licenses: B2B Finpal, EthisCrowd, Fundaztic, Quickash, FundedByMe, and Funding Societies.

- Digital investment management framework

  This framework was established in 2017. Its focus is on licensing and the requirements for offering automated discretionary portfolio management services to investors. In essence, the technology capabilities and competent people must be in place in the company. The technology or algorithm can be outsourced, but accountability still falls under the framework. However, as of now, no licenses have been awarded to any operators.

- Companies Commission of Malaysia (CCM)

  The CCM incorporates companies and registers business while providing information to the public. It began operation on 16 April 2002.

Beside the regulatory bodies' initiatives on fintech, there are other institutions that help to promote fintech industries, including:

i) Fintech Association of Malaysia (FAOM)

FAOM was established in October 2016 by a group of parties involved in fintech, community leaders, government agencies, and like-minded people, with the main objective of being a voice for the industry.

ii) Malaysian Global Innovation & Creativity Centre (MaGIC)

MaGIC was launched on 27 April 2014 by US President Barack Obama and the Prime Minister of Malaysia Seri Najib Tun Razak. Through the Global Accelerator Program (GAP), three participants of the program are from fintech – MHUB, Direct Lending, and Swapit in the mortgage management platform, money lending services, and currency exchange services respectively (Star, July 2017).

iii) Malaysian Digital Economy Corporation (MDEC)

This government linked agency has established a dedicated team for fintech and start-ups.

iv) Cradle Fund

This fund was established under the Ministry of Finance and has raised RM 1.3 million through the ECF platform PitchIn for fintech start-ups. Its programs include:

- Cradle Investment Program 300 (CIP300)
- A preseed program which provides financial and value-added assistance up to RM 300,000
- Direct Equity 800 (DEQ800)
- Equity investment up to RM 800,000 for local tech start-ups
- Angle Tax Incentive

- Tax deduction up to RM 500,000 off personal income tax for investment in Malaysian technology start-ups
- Coach & Grow Program
- A program intended to bring together support and to fortify technology entrepreneurships in fintech

v) Supercharger

Based in Hong Kong, this fintech accelerator, in collaboration with Malaysia Digital Economy Corporation (MDEC), Standard Chartered Bank, and Allianz Malaysia, has selected ten start-ups for its first cohort. The chosen start-ups are in regulatory technology (RegTech, Capnovum, Know-Your-Customer), digital identity (Cekk), cognitive analytics (MyFinB), insurance technology (InsurTech, Neosurance, RegTech), wealth tech (Neuroprofiler), artificial intelligence and chatbots (Pand.ai), big data analytics (Pulse ID), cyber-security (Solus, InsurTech), software as a service (Springday), and payment hubs (Tramonex) (Star, September 2017).

3.3.4 Malaysian banks' response to fintech

In the Malaysian context, Islamic banks have led in fintech, and several introduced the Islamic Interbank Investment Platform (IAP) in 2015. This is the first Islamic fintech solution on an investment platform offered by a consortium of six Islamic Banks. This online investment platform helps secure funding for projects, linking individuals, companies, and rating agencies (Star, July 2016). Some of the initiatives taken by major Malaysian local banks towards fintech are presented in more detail in Table 3.16.

Table 3.16 Malaysian bank initiatives on fintech

Bank	*Initiatives on fintech*
Maybank	Maybank has established partnerships with payment fintech firms such as Alipay and Samsung Pay. It also recently launched the fintech Open API platform Maybank Sandbox. Maybank has introduced a digital wallet called MaybankPay, followed by Maybank QRPay (cashless mobile payment using QR codes). It organizes the annual Maybank Fintech program with the main theme of "Go-to-market." This annual program focused on partnerships among participants which leverage each other's resources (Fong, February 2018).

(*Continued*)

Table 3.16 (Continued)

Bank	*Initiatives on fintech*
CIMB Bank	CIMB has set up a fintech unit and a partnership with Startupbootcamp, a company that provides support for early-stage technology founders. Some of the initiatives taken by CIMB include introducing CIMB EVA (a chat bot programmed to simulate conversations between two people), Rekening Ponsel (allowing most transactions to be carried through a mobile number), and Beat Banking (a collaboration between CIMB Thai and Advance Info Service Public Company Limited [AIS] that aims to develop a suite of new banking solutions for mobile phones).
RHB Bank	As the fourth largest bank in Malaysia, RHB has conducted a Fintech Hackathon with Startupbootcamp. The second of these was held from 28 to 30 July 2017. During that program, the 11 best entries were selected for the start-up program. RHB also works with two leading fintech companies in Malaysia, MoneyMatch and Funding Societies (Fong, February 2018).
Hong Leong Bank	Hong Leong has introduced the Hong Leong Bank Launchpad in collaboration with Cradle, Malaysian Business Angel Network (MBAN), and WTF Accelerator. On July 2017, five start-ups were selected, including Blinkware Technology, CapitalBay, Kakitangan.com, Propsocial, and Sales Candy International. In 2016, HLB also deployed cognitive banking technology with IBM Watson (Fong, February 2018). For future, the bank is planning technology such as augmented and virtual reality, robotics, blockchain, and application programs (Fong, February 2018).
Public Bank	There is no clear indication of the fintech involvement of Public Bank. No major media announcements have been made regarding fintech. Historically, this bank is known as being more conservative about technology (Fong, February 2018).
Am Bank	There is some indication that AM is paying attention to fintech. It has made several media announcements regarding its willingness to participate with fintech (Fong, February 2018).

References

Journal articles

Ahmed, I., Forde, B., Laplanche, R., Mitra, A., Bay, N.P., and Scandurra, A. (2015). The fintech revolution: How innovators are using technology to take on the world of finance. *London Business School Review*, *3*.

Bank Negara Malaysia (1999). *The Central Bank and the Financial System in Malaysia: A Decade of Change (1989–1999)*. Kuala Lumpur: Bank Negara Malaysia.

CGI. (2014). Understanding financial consumers in the digital era: A survey and perspective on emerging financial consumer trends. *CGI Groups*. Retrieved from

https://www.cgi.com/sites/default/files/pdf/br_fs_consumersurveyreport_final_july_2014.pdf
Diamond, D.W., and Rajan, R.G. (2001). Liquidity risk, liquidity creation, and financial fragility: A theory of banking. *Journal of Political Economy*, *109*(2), 287–327.
Fong, V. (2018, February 19). What are Malaysia's top 5 banks doing about fintech? Fintech Malaysia. Retrieved from https://fintechnews.my/16580/banking/bank-fintech-malaysia/
Hendricks, D., and Hirtle, B. (1997). Bank capital requirements for market risk: The internal models approach. *Economic Policy Review*, *3*(4), 1–22. Retrieved from https://www.newyorkfed.org/research/epr/97v03n4/9712hend.html
Ibrahim, M. (2016, May). Future of Islamic finance: Delivering actions today for a sustainable tomorrow. *Governor's Keynote Address at the Global Islamic Finance Forum 5.0*. Retrieved from www.bnm.gov.my/index.php?ch=en_speech&pg=en_speech&ac=690&lang=en
Jones, A. (2017, April). China: The world's new fintech leader. *International Banker*.
KPMG. (2017, April). Setting course in a disrupted marketplace: The digitally-enabled bank of the future. Retrieved from https://kpmg.com
Mahomed, Z., and Mohamad, S. (2016). Disruptors: Financial innovation and riding the Fintech wave. *Centre of Islamic Asset and Wealth Management*, 1–4. Retrieved from http://www.inceif.org/archive/wp-content/uploads/2018/02/Bulletin-Vol.2-article-2.pdf
McIntyre, A. (2017, August). How banks can win with rewards programs by using APIs. *Forbes*.
Omar, M. (2017, October 11). Fintech and entrepreneurship. *Assistant Governor's Opening Remarks at Islamic Fintech Dialogue 2017*. Retrieved from www.bnm.gov.my/index.php?ch=en_speech&pg=en_speech&ac=764&lang=en
Ong, M. (2016, November). Are financial institutions in Malaysia ready for fintech? *Digital News Asia*.
Pikri, E. (2017). A new centre in KL is part of a USD40 mil expansion, thanks to Blockchain. Retrieved from https://vulcanpost.com/615237/blockchain-fintech-malaysia-nem-bitcoin-future/
Pollari, I. (2016). The rise of fintech: Opportunities and challenges. *The Finsia Journal of Applied Finance*, *3*, 15–21.
Santomero, A.M. (1997). Commercial bank risk management: An analysis of the process. *Journal of Financial Services Research*, *12*(2–3), 83–115.
Star. (2016, July 21). Regulatory framework for fintech in Q4. Retrieved from www.thestar.com.my/business/business-news/2016/07/21/bank-negara-regulatory-framework-for-fintech-in-q4/
Star. (2017, July 10). Becoming a global hub for startups. Retrieved from www.thestar.com.my/metro/smebiz/news/2017/07/10/becoming-a-global-hub-for-startups/
Star. (2017, September 27). SuperCharger chooses 10 start-ups for its accelerator programme. Retrieved from www.thestar.com.my/business/business-news/2017/09/27/supercharger-chooses-10-startups-for-its-accelerator-programme/
Wollan, R., Davis, P., De Angelis, F., and Quiring, K. (2017). Seeing beyond the loyalty illusion: It's time you invest more wisely. *Accenture Strategy*, 1–7. Retrieved from https://www.accenture.com/t00010101T000000Z__w__/gb-en/_acnmedia/

PDF-43/Accenture-Strategy-GCPR-Customer-Loyalty.pdf%22%20%5Cl%20%22zoom=50

Yurcan, B. (2016, April). How will APIs change banking? PNC looks within for the answer. *American Banker*.

List of reports

Bank International Settlement (2004). International convergence of capital measurement and capital standards: A revised framework. Comprehensive Version. Retrieved from https://www.bis.org/publ/bcbs04a.htm

Bank Negara Malaysia (2008). Risk assessment of the financial system. Retrieved from https://www.bnm.gov.my/files/.../fsps/en/.../cp01_002_whitebox.pdf

Bank Negara Malaysia Annual Report 1998. Retrieved from www.bnm.gov.my/index.php?ch=en_publication&pg=en_ar&ac=3&lang=en

Bank Negara Malaysia Annual Report 1999. Retrieved from www.bnm.gov.my/index.php?ch=en_publication&pg=en_ar&ac=3&lang=en

Bank Negara Malaysia Annual Report 2004. Retrieved from www.bnm.gov.my/index.php?ch=en_publication&pg=en_ar&ac=3&lang=en

Bank Negara Malaysia Annual Report 2005. Retrieved from www.bnm.gov.my/index.php?ch=en_publication&pg=en_ar&ac=3&lang=en

Bank Negara Malaysia Annual Report 2006. Retrieved from www.bnm.gov.my/index.php?ch=en_publication&pg=en_ar&ac=3&lang=en

Bank Negara Malaysia Annual Report 2007. Retrieved from www.bnm.gov.my/index.php?ch=en_publication&pg=en_ar&ac=3&lang=en

Bank Negara Malaysia Annual Report 2008. Retrieved from www.bnm.gov.my/index.php?ch=en_publication&pg=en_ar&ac=3&lang=en

Bank Negara Malaysia Annual Report 2009. Retrieved from www.bnm.gov.my/index.php?ch=en_publication&pg=en_ar&ac=3&lang=en

Bank Negara Malaysia Annual Report 2010. Retrieved from http://www.bnm.gov.my/files/publication/ar/en/2010/cp05.pdf

Bank Negara Malaysia Annual Report 2012. Retrieved from www.bnm.gov.my/index.php?ch=en_publication&pg=en_ar&ac=3&lang=en

Financial Stability and Payment Systems Report 2011. Retrieved from http://www.bnm.gov.my/files/publication/fsps/en/2011/cp01.pdf

Financial Stability and Payment Systems Report 2016. Retrieved from www.bnm.gov.my/index.php?ch=en_publication&pg=en_fspr&ac=11

4 Bank bailout efficacy

Aidil Rizal Shahrin, Chan Sok-Gee, and Rozaimah Zainudin

4.1 Prior studies and theories

4.1.1 Moral hazard, risk-taking, and the theories

A moral hazard is often associated with bank risk-taking behaviour, which can be used to explain the occurrence of banking crises over the past two decades. Banks take excessive risks, which lead to financial instability, eventually resulting in banking crises. The moral hazard behaviour of the banks is partly to be blamed as the outcome of the 2008 global financial crisis (GFC) which resulted in bank failure in the US market and in developed countries around the globe. To date (October 2017), the Federal Deposit Insurance Corporation (FDIC) has reported 529 bank failures since 2007.

Moral hazards in the banking system can be explained using two competing hypotheses: competition-fragility and competition-stability. The competition-fragility hypothesis gained ground in the banking industry following the theoretical work of Marcus (1984) and Keeley (1990) on the charter value hypothesis. Saunders and Wilson (1996) found support for Keeley's results in the US banking industry from 1973 to 1992. This was further supported by Demsetz, Saidenberg and Strahan (1996), who provided similar evidence of the charter value hypothesis in the US banking industry: using a sample of US banks between 1986 and 1994, they found that lower charter values of banks lead to increased bank risk-taking activities.

Keeley (1990) also highlighted that competition increases the pressure on profit, which leads to higher risk-taking among banking institutions. Hannan and Prager (1998) found that liberalization of interstate branching and operations increased competition in deposit markets in the US, hurting the profitability of banks. This is also consistent with the study of Shaffer (1998), who found that competition involves new entries into the banking industry, which increases loan losses and results in high levels of information asymmetry. Allen and Gale (2000) found that the lower market power of banks significantly reduced profitability, leading the banks to invest in riskier assets to compensate. Allen and Gale (2004) and Boyd, DeNicolo and Smith (2004) also found evidence that competitive banking systems lead to financial fragility through reductions in charter value as a result of lower profitability. This is consistent with the study of Martinez-Miera and Repullo (2010), which found that competition reduces the interest income of banks more than the reduction of nonperforming loans (NPLs). The dominant effect of the reduction in interest income is to increase the risk-taking behaviour of the banking institutions, further leading to bank failure. This is consistent with the study of Hellmann, Murdock and Stiglitz (2000) that examined the relationships between competition for deposits, risk-taking, and regulations. Their results suggest that the removal of interest ceilings on deposits reduces the charter value of the banks and motivates risk-taking behaviour.

Besides lower profitability due to intense competition in the banking industry, Boot and Greenbaum (1993) and Allen and Gale (2000) also highlighted that competition reduces informational rent and the relationships between banks and borrowers. This reduces the incentives for banks to properly screen their borrowers, thus leading to higher risk-taking. Cetorelli and Peretto (2000) also found that concentrated banking sectors have reduced information asymmetry due to proper screening of quality borrowers. One reason for the reduction in proper screening may due to high monitoring costs, as suggested by Caminal and Matutes (2002). They found that a reduction in credit rationing increases the probability of failure in the banking industry. This supports the study by Boot and Thakor (2000), who found that larger banks in more concentrated markets practice credit rationing that increases financial soundness. Vives (2011) suggests that competition resulted in banking instability, because it worsens the coordination problem of depositors on the liability side.

Diamond (1984), Boyd and Prescott (1986), and Williamson (1986) also offer more evidence for the competition-fragility hypothesis, in support of more concentration. They found that less competition makes larger banks capitalize their assets better through economies of scale and scope, as well as better diversification. This is supported by Paroush (1995), who found that US banks achieve higher stability due to increases in market power as a result of diversification gains from mergers. In a similar vein, Craig and Santos (1997) also found that banks increased in post-merger profitability and reduced post-merger risk, on a sample of 256 acquisitions by US bank holding companies. This is consistent with the results of Boyd and Runkle (1993) in their analysis of 122 US bank holding companies between 1971 and 1990. Their results suggest that larger banks benefitted from diversification without tolerance for higher banking risks. Carletti, Hartmann and

Spangnolo (2007) also found that merged banks decrease their reserve with better diversification effects, which modifies the distribution of bank sizes and liquidity needs, leading to better bank stability.

Empirical studies of US banking that support the competition-fragility hypothesis include those of Paroush (1995), Craig and Santos (1997), Boyd and Runkle (1993), Demsetz, Saidenberg and Strahan (1996), Saunders and Wilson (1996), Cetorelli and Peretto (2000), Boot and Thakor (2000), Boyd et al. (2004), Carletti, Hartmann and Spangnolo (2007), Berger, Klapper and Turk-Ariss (2009), Brunnermeier, Dong and Palia (2011), Schaeck and Cihak (2012), and Beck, Jonghe and Schepens (2013). Evidence from international banking can be found in the studies of Amidu and Wolfe (2013) and Jiménez, Lopez and Saurina (2013).

The competition-stability hypothesis was first highlighted by Mishkin (1999). It states that larger banks are inefficient because they are more likely to receive public guarantees during bank runs. This creates a "too-big-to-fail" scenario which increases the chance that banks will engage in risky investment because they are protected by the government's safety net. Besides, less competition in a more concentrated market gives freedom for the banks to act: banks may thus take excessive risks to earn higher returns and hence become involved in moral hazard behaviour that distorts the stability of the financial system (Uhde and Heimeshoff, 2009). Caminal and Matutes (2002) examined the effects of concentration on bank fragility. Their results suggest that monopoly banks charge higher loan rates, ration credit less, and have higher probability of failure as a result of moral hazard behaviour, as has also been suggested by Mishkin (1999). This is supported by De Nicolo and Loukoianova (2007), who found higher levels of systemic risk to be associated with less competitive banking systems. In addition, De Nicolo and Loukoianova (2007) further found a positive and significant relationship between bank concentration and the probability of bank failure, especially in state-owned banks in 133 industrialized countries. Further evidence has been provided by Uhde and Heimeshoff (2009) in their analysis of the banking industry in Europe.

Boyd and De Nicolo (2005) and Mirzaei, Moore and Liu (2013) also argued that banks operating in a more competitive environment offer lower lending rates to borrowers, eventually lowering the cost of borrowing for firms and hence lowering the credit risk on loan portfolios that contributes significantly to banking stability. Koskela and Stenbacka (2000) found that competition contributes to bank stability because lower lending rates and greater investment in mean-shifting investment technologies reduce the bankruptcy risk of the borrowers. This was reaffirmed by Boyd, De Nicolo and Jalal (2009), who found that the default risk of borrowers is highly correlated with bank failures. In addition, healthy competition increases financial depth (Rice and Strahan, 2010) and promotes efficient information flow (Claessens and Laeven, 2005), which eventually reduce the information asymmetry, thus enhancing the allocation of resources in the market and consequently leading to a more stable banking system.

On the other hand, Schaeck, Cihak and Wolfe (2009) argued that the relationship between competition and risk-taking can be mitigated if banks have higher capital buffers when they operate in a more competitive environment. Beck, Jonghe and Schepens (2013) found that market power reduces this soundness, noting that this relationship worsened during the financial crisis. In line with Schaeck, Cihak and Wolfe (2009), Beck, Jonghe and Schepens (2013) found that competition has greater impact on bank stability in countries with stricter activity restrictions, lower systemic fragility, better developed stock exchanges, more generous deposit insurance, and more effective systems for sharing credit information.

To summarize, there is strong empirical evidence for both the more concentration (less competition) and less concentration (more competition) theories in relation to moral hazard and risk-taking behaviour in the banking industry. There are thus no conclusive results, despite continuous study of the bailout programs implemented in the developed and developing economies.

4.2 The Malaysian experience

4.2.1 The trigger: the Asian financial crisis

4.2.1.1 Prior to the crisis

Asian economies were the centre of attention in the 1990s. Signs of economic success were numerous: exports were expanding, standard of living was rising with high GDPs, prudent fiscal policies, and high household saving rate, all of which pointed to Asia being an ideal destination for foreign investment. With all the success stories, coupled with the liberalization of financial markets, the Asian economy attracted heavy capital inflows during this decade. This was further enhanced by the relatively weaker growth of GDP in most industrial economies, which led to accommodative monetary policies and low interest rates, resulting in a decline in asset yields. Most inflows were in terms of short-term debts denominated in yen and dollar, causing currencies to appreciate, since many were linked to the dollar. In 1996, there were USD $136 billion (5.2% of Asian GDP) in net private capital inflows, with most of the short-term capital flows coming from European and Japanese banks (IMF, 1999b). The net private capital flows in the countries most affected by the crisis – Thailand, Indonesia, Korea, Malaysia, and the Philippines – were USD $32 billion in 1993, USD $33 billion in 1994, and USD $63 billion per year in 1995 and 1996 (IMF, 1999b). However, these inflows began to decelerate after 1996, with an increase in real GDP growth rate in the US and the Federal Reserve increasing the short-term interest rate (IMF, 1999b). The same pattern also occurred in Europe and Japan in 1996.

Radelet and Sachs suggested that these massive capital inflows into Asian economies were the main cause of the Asian financial crisis (Radelet and Sachs, 1998). They pointed to four factors that contributed to these inflows: i) high growth that gave confidence to foreign investors; ii) deregulation of financial sectors without adequate supervision, especially in Thailand; iii) nominal exchange rates that were effectively pegged to US dollar or underwent only limited variation from it; and iv) governments providing statutory incentives to foreign borrowing. At the centre of these authors' thesis is the role of banking sector. This inflow fuelled lending booms, and with inadequate supervision, resulted in excessive risk-taking in the banking sector. As noted by Das (1999), the growth of bank credit beginning in 1992 in Asian economies would be considered excessive by any standard.

In fact, the massive capital inflow into Asian economies was partly due to the liberalization of financial markets. Kaminsky and Schmukler (2008) indicated that most Asian countries began to liberalize their financial market in the early 1990s. Korea, Thailand, and Indonesia fully liberalized their financial markets prior to the crisis, while Indonesia began this process in January 1991. Malaysia went through multiple rounds of liberalization, beginning in 1973, after the country accepted its obligation under Article VIII in November 1968; further liberalization of controls occurred in 1986–1987 and 1994–1996 (IMF, 1999b). In this second round of liberalization, the focus was on boosting export-oriented activities, as a consequence of the 1985 recession. Malaysia subsequently focused on an industrialization strategy, moving from import substitution to export orientation (IMF, 1999a). For this reason, later on in the 1980s, Malaysia adopted a trade policy to improve the competitiveness of its exports, with emphasis on the liberalization of essential imports of capital goods and intermediate goods. Accordingly, the Malaysian ringgit was allowed to depreciate beginning September 1994 (IMF, 1999a). Earlier, the ringgit's exchange rate had been determined on the basis of a composite basket of currencies of Malaysia's trading partners. The ringgit was not rigidly pegged to this basket, but was permitted a narrow fluctuation relative to it (IMF, 1999a).

4.2.1.2 Eve of the crisis

Signs of distress were visible right before the crisis struck. In Thailand, the current account deficit rose rapidly, from 5.6% of GDP in 1994 to 8.5% in 1996 (Das, 1999). This deficit created a growing asset bubble in Thailand.

The Thai property market had provided high return since the mid-1960s. Due to the dollar-linked exchange rate system, the Thai baht was overvalued, and was thus substantially financed by foreign currency loans and the property boom, resulting in excess construction (Das, 1999). However, in 1996, Thailand's exports declined. Consequently, finance companies faced cash flow difficulties due to their heavy investment in the real estate market, where the price had been stagnant, and was now coupled with excess supply. The government's bailout of these finance companies worsened the situation, attracting attacks on the baht peg (Das, 1999). The baht came under repeated speculative attack, causing the central bank to lose its reserve in attempting to defend it (Das, 1999).

Korea and the Philippines also experienced large account deficits prior to the crisis. The increase in Korea's current deficit began in 1996, which resulted in the accumulation of short-term debt. The growth rate of industrial production in 1996 was half that of the previous year. The chaebols had high debt–equity ratios and their creditor banks were destabilized by the high chance of bankruptcy (Das, 1999). Although the Philippines' macroeconomic condition was encouraging, due to reform under the supervision of the International Monetary Fund (IMF, 1999b), this country also experienced a large current account deficit with an overvalued Philippine peso and a lending boom that led to unsound investment (Das, 1999).

Internally, the stock markets of the crisis-hit economies were not spared from speculative attack, which began in 1996. In Malaysia and the Philippines, the stock price indices were 52% and 48%, respectively, in terms of local currency, between June 1997 and January 1998. Indonesia suffered much worse with an 80% drop in its stock index in the same period (Das, 1999)

On the other hand, Malaysia entered the crisis with generally stronger economic fundamentals than the severely crisis-stricken countries: prudent fiscal policy, higher growth, and its financial institutions generally had fewer NPLs and higher capital. There was also a surge in public investment before the crisis, partly related to prestigious infrastructure projects. Moreover, in 1996, Malaysia's interest rate was high, which further attracted short-term capital inflows. This occurred as the government imposed limits on non-commercial offer-side swap transactions, which had resulted in a wide spread between domestic and offshore interest (IMF, 1999a). However, this flow of ringgit funds from the onshore to the offshore resulted in contraction of the economy.

4.2.1.3 The crisis

When the economy experiences steep currency depreciation, a sharp drop in GDP, and a steep increase in interest rate, these are signals that the economy is in financial crisis. On July 2, 1997, the Thai baht was unpegged from the dollar (World Bank, 1998). The crisis originated from Thailand and spread initially to the Philippines and Malaysia, and later to Indonesia and Korea. Singapore, Hong Kong, and Taiwan were also affected, though not as severely as the five badly hit countries. During that week, the baht depreciated by about 15%. The Bangkok stock market plummeted by 30% in 1997. This steep depreciation affected not only the baht: the Indonesian rupiah, the Philippine peso, and the Malaysian ringgit also faced the same scenario. Depreciation in the peso and rupiah accelerated after 11 July and 17 August, although they were gradually depreciated during the week the baht was unpegged from the dollar. By January 1998, the nominal exchange rates of all the severely crisis-stricken countries had depreciated significantly against the dollar – by 79%, 52%, 42%, and 36%, respectively for the rupiah, baht, ringgit, and peso. The Korean won had depreciated by 41% in January 1998. Besides the currency depreciation during the crisis, credit also tightened as financial institutions suffered accumulated nonperforming loans, which increased the possibility of insolvency and liquidity issues.

The liberalization of capital account seems to be one of the main causes of the Asian financial crisis. This economic policy, coupled with problems in the financial system, such as poor supervision and regulation, caused financial institutions to become involved in excessive risk. As argued by Radelet and Sachs (1998) and D'Arista and Griffith-Jones (1998), large capital inflows always create a policy dilemma – especially if volatile, unsustainable, or poorly utilized. However, Radelet and Sachs (1998) did not discount the importance of the capital flows in generating economic growth where it must be channelled to productive investment activities.

Similarly, Stiglitz (2002) echoed the same idea regarding the cause of the crisis. He suggested that the key to the crisis was the liberalization of capital accounts. He emphasized that such liberalization can impose enormous risks, even for countries that possess strong banks and a mature stock market, which the Asian counties lacked. Wang (2007) instead examined the popular explanation of the financial crisis: cronyism, exchange rate policy, weak macroeconomics fundamentals, open capital account, poor regulation and supervision of financial institutions, lack of transparency, and weak banks. He concluded that premature capital account liberalization was the main cause of financial crises, including the Asian crisis. Wang took used China as an example of a country that controls and monitors the pace and sequence of financial liberalization and of domestic financial regulation. In China, capital accounts are strictly controlled, and renminbi are not convertible for capital account transactions, which limits the possibility of renminbi leaving the country during a crisis. In essence, Wang suggested delaying the liberalization of capital account or maintaining capital controls.

In contrast, Eichengreen and Mussa (1998) felt that the root cause was not the liberalization of capital account, but rather the inadequacy of prudential supervision and regulation. They argued that the role of the liberalization of the capital account was only that it increased the impact of the crisis.

4.2.2 The Malaysian regulator's response to the Asian financial crisis

The Malaysian government responded to the crisis in January 1998 with the formation of the National Economic Action Council (NEAC), a consultative body to the Malaysian cabinet. The main role of NEAC was to propose policies and operational measures to curb the crisis. In doing so, it prepared the National Economy Recovery Plan (NERP). In particular, this policy proposed the implementation of capital controls: foreigners would not be allowed to sell stocks or repatriate funds until 12 months after purchasing (IMF, 1999a). The restriction was replaced in February 1999 with exit levies, which decreased with the duration of investment. This levy gave an important signal to foreign investors since instilling investor confidence lay at the heart of the crisis (IMF, 1999a). With this control, the government could lower the interest rate to counteract the recession without causing the ringgit to collapse (IMF, 1999a). Kaplan and Rodrik (2001) compared Malaysia's capital control to that of Korea and Thailand, which were under the recovery program of the IMF. They found that the Malaysian capital control was much more successful, helping speed up recovery as compared to Korea and Thailand. Malaysia also managed to reduce the interest rate to single digits, while the offshore ringgit paid interest rates of 20% to 40%.

The ringgit was also officially pegged at RM3.80 to a dollar and large denomination notes were demonetized. After the pegging announcement, Malaysian stock prices fell steeply, but the value of ringgit was unaffected (IMF, 1999a). The Malaysian government also announced that all ringgits held outside Malaysia had to be returned, so that ringgit trading would occur entirely within Malaysia's borders (Das, 1999).

In dealing with rising NPLs in the banking system, the NERP suggested the establishment of asset management companies (AMC) and special purpose vehicles (SPVs). In addition, a Corporate Debt Restructuring Committee (CDRC) was established in August 1998 to focus on financial and corporate restructuring.

The aim of AMC was to deal with financial institutions' rising NPLs: they constituted 2–3% of loans between March and September 1997, but reached double-digits by July 1998 (Danaharta, 2006). In order to acquire the NPLs from the financial institutions, Pengurusan Danaharta Nasional Berhad ("Danaharta") was established in June 1998. There are two extreme approaches to dealing with NPLs: a rapid disposition agency that takes over the assets of the bank and disposes of them quickly, and a warehousing agency that takes over NPLs and warehouses them (Danaharta, 2006). In contrast, the AMC's target was to maximize recovery by managing NPLs in its portfolio on an account-to-account basis (Danaharta, 2006). There are two main reasons for this choice (Danaharta, 2006):

i) the NPLs suffered from structural issues, which required business solution rather than loans;
ii) the NPLs are chunky, with 2,000 to 3,000 accounts valued at RM5 million or more.

The government provided RM3 billion in initial funds for Danaharta, which came in stages. In the interim, the operational funding was borrowed from the Employment Provident Fund (EPF) and Khazanah Nasional Berhad (Danaharta, 2006). All the loans needed to be discounted before being sold to Danaharta; the initial estimate was RM25 billion, but turned out to be much lower than anticipated. It should be noted that Danaharta was intended as a finite-lived institution that was intended to last less than ten years (in fact it existed between 20 June 1998 and 31 December 2005). It was expected to recover 58% of the NPLs, which it achieved by 30 September 2005 (Danaharta, 2006).

Danamodal Nasional Berhad (Danamodal) was established as an SPV in August 1998 to recapitalize financial institutions. The idea was that Danamodal would inject fresh capital into financial institutions so that they could meet their capital requirements. Before the capital was injected, the existing shareholders needed to absorb their initial losses. Accordingly, an independent valuation by Goldman Sachs or Salomon Smith Barney was conducted, followed by a review by the supervision and regulation department of BNM (IMF, 1999a). Danamodal also had representation on the boards of directors of all the financial institutions that they recapitalized. With funding of RM11 billion, RM6.2 billion was injected into 11 financial institutions, constituting one-fifth of financial institution assets (IMF, 1999a).

Danaharta and Danamodal's primary funding was through the issuance of zero-coupon bonds. The bonds issued by Danaharta carry an explicit government guarantee and the issuance of up to RM15 billion (face value) was authorized; RM1.5 billion capital was provided by the Ministry of Finance. The bonds issued by Danamodal possessed an implied government guarantee, since the body is owned by BNM. Danamodal's bonds were issued in conjunction with a lower statutory reserve requirement from the BNM (Danaharta, 2006).

In addition to financial institutions, BNM also realized the need to implement corporate structure simultaneously with the financial institutions. For this reason, the CRDC was established. Its main goals were (IMF, 1999a):

i) to facilitate discussion between borrowers and financial institutions with the aim of expediting and voluntarily restructuring debts;
ii) to facilitate debt restructuring of large borrowers (more than RM50 million) under the condition that the business were still viable;
iii) to employ the London approach to debt workout.

Although Danamodal, Danaharta, and CRDC were governed by their respective operational frameworks, they were complementary and all their activities were coordinated by a steering committee chaired by the governor of BNM (IMF, 1999a).

Besides these approaches, consolidation of banking institutions through merger also took place in 1999 to resolve problems associated with smaller and weaker banks. This was conducted with the aim of enhancing the role of banks as financial intermediaries, which required the institutions involved to be more resilient, efficient, and competitive (BNM, 1999). However, the operations some of banking institutions – namely, Kewangan Bersatu Berhad, MBf Finance Berhad, Sabah Finance Berhad, and Sime Merchant Bankers Berhad – fell under the direct control of BNM, as they had suffered substantial losses from high NPL levels, which rapidly eroded their capital (BNM, 1999). This also helped avoid any systematic failure in banking institutions. In addition, Kewangan Bersatu Berhad and Sabah Finance Berhad merged respectively with Mayban Finance Berhad and Multi-Purpose Bank Berhad as part of the rescue operations (BNM, 1999). Likewise, two domestic commercial banks, Sime Bank Berhad and Bank Bumiputra Berhad, merged respectively with RHB Bank Berhad and Bank of Commerce (M) Berhad, again due to substantial losses made by these two commercial banks through high NPLs. The mergers were completed on 30 June 1999 and 30 September 1999, respectively.

In essence, all domestic banking sectors in Malaysia were given flexibility to form their own merger groups and to choose their own leader for the mergers, with the merger exercises needing to be finalized by the end of December 2000 (BNM Annual Report, 1999). As a result, ten banking groups were formed, with the leaders of the mergers being:

i) Malayan Banking Berhad
ii) RHB Bank Berhad
iii) Public Bank Berhad
iv) Bumiputra-Commerce Bank Berhad

v) Multi-Purpose Bank Berhad
vi) Hong Leong Bank Berhad
vii) Perwira Affin Bank Berhad
viii) Arab-Malaysian Bank Berhad
ix) Southern Bank Berhad
x) EON Bank Berhad

This resulted in a reduction in the number of domestic banking institutions from 54 to 29 (BNM Annual Report, 1999).

4.3 The US experience

4.3.1 The trigger: the global financial crisis

4.3.1.1 The US housing loan market

The US housing loan market grew at an extraordinary pace during the 2000s. One of the major contributors to this growth was the introduction of a securitization concept based on more flexible loans than were usual for US households. This subprime lending was designed for customers with low credit scores and low down payments, and was less strict in its income documentation requirements. It thus extended mortgages to those who would have had very limited opportunity to apply for conventional housing loans (Verick and Islam, 2010). Subprime mortgages also allowed refinancing of existing housing loans for extra liquidity and a lower interest rate (Mayer and Pence, 2008). Mayer and Pence's (2008) data, generated from the Loan Performance and Housing Mortgage Disclosure Act, shows a dramatic upward trend in subprime lending from 1998 to 2006. The loan performance measurement was at 300,000 in 1998 and grew to 1.5 million in 2006, increasing by a factor of five within eight years. Furthermore, the Housing Mortgage Disclosure Act data also shows that the US subprime market peaked in 2005, with 3 million mortgages in that year. The growth further signalled an increase in the number of borrowers of substandard quality; this deterioration in quality would lead to enormous overdue payments upon any increase in the subprime interest rate. Hence, the market did not have an accurate total risk exposure regarding these mortgage subprime lenders. In addition, the mortgage subprime lenders were outside the Federal Reserve's remit, not being regulated in the same way as conventional banks.

The huge demand from these subprime borrowers pushed the housing market growth rate dramatically up, creating a US housing bubble. This bubble could be seen in the unsustainable overvaluation of real property relative to income and other measurements of affordability. Overvalued prices reached the maximum and subsequently led to a reduction in housing prices to an all-time low, surpassing the level of debt created by the mortgages based on these overvalued properties. The overvalued properties then attracted more subprime borrowers to take more risk upon themselves in order to obtain greater return on their investments.

The cause of this bubble could possibly be traced back to the very low interest rate. The Federal Reserve board reduced the short-term interest rate from 6.5% to 1% in 2001 (Bianco, 2008), which in turn affected the long-term rate. With an extremely low interest rate for long-term borrowing, mortgages become more appealing and more consumers are likely to seek mortgages to purchase a new home or to refinance a home in order to take advantage of this low interest scenario. This all-time low interest rate created great demand for new houses and further increased property values. Refinancing created stronger liquidity positions and lower loan repayments. Greenspan has contrarily indicated that it was an increase in global savings that pushed the interest rate to an all-time low and further inflated the housing value globally. However, much academic writing suggests that it was in fact the all-time low interest rate that inflated the housing bubble in the US (see Elmendorf, 2007; Holt, 2009).

Apart from low interest rates, Taylor (2009) has suggested that the excessively loose monetary policy implemented by the US government may have been another contributor to the collapse of US financial institutions. A low interest rate and loose financial regulation made many US banks take more leverage with the aim of achieving greater return on their investments. At the same time, the global imbalance between the saving influxes from surplus countries (China) to deficit economics (US) further worsened the global financial crisis.

4.3.1.2 Subprime mortgage crisis

The rapid growth of these securitized mortgage loans was no ordinary growth rate: subprime lenders or originators sold these subprime loans to other financial institutions (investment bankers) using an originate-to-distribute business model. With the proceeds of the sale, they continued to offer new subprime loans (see Figure 4.1). Hence, the subprime default risk had now been transferred to the purchasing financial institutions, which issued Mortgage-Backed Securities (MBS) by transferring these subprime loans into structured investment vehicles (SIV). These MBS instruments disassociate the original asset owners from the risk that arose from the poor credit assessment, further increasing the risk for these MBS issuers (Mah-Hui, 2008). MBS securities were ranked into Senior/AAA, Junior/Mezzanine and Noninvestment Grade/Subordinate tranches based on comprehensive

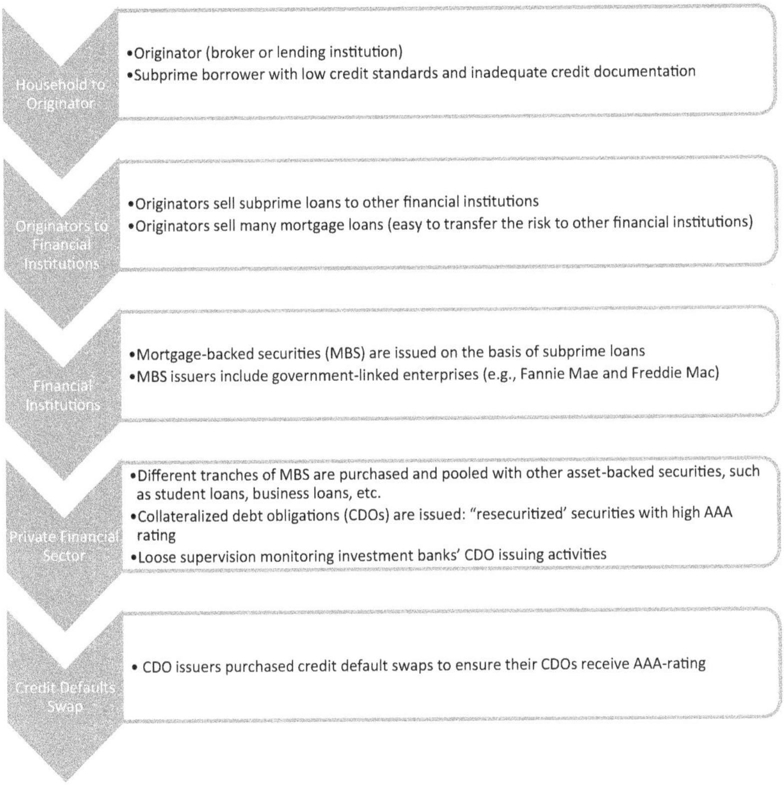

Figure 4.1 Risk transmission process from subprime borrower to private financial sectors

Source: Adapted from Baily, Litan and Johnson (2008) and Astley et al. (2009)

risk analysis and on a set of assumptions. However, the risk analysis for this tranche grading was not done properly.

More MBS securities were issued to the market and transferred to private financial sectors in the form of collateralized debt obligations (CDOs). CDO issuers combined these MBS tranches with other type of loans, including business loans, education loans, automobile loans, and others into CDO "resecuritized" securities (Mah-Hui, 2008). Credit default swap contracts were purchased by the CDO issuers to increase the CDO's rating to AAA (Baily, Litan and Johnson, 2008; Astley et al., 2009). The volume of CDOs traded grew from USD $125 billion in 2004 to USD $350 billion in 2006 (Mah-Hui, 2008), further increasing enormously to USD $500 billion in 2007

(Crotty, 2009). Figure 4.1 describes the risk transmission process from the subprime borrowers to other private financial sectors in the form of CDOs.

The Federal Reserve board made 17 changes in the US interest rate, from 1% to 5.25% from 2004 to 2006. Further necessary corrections were made, as it was decided to not increase the rate further when it became apparent that housing values were decelerating very rapidly with the increase in interest rate. Consumer spending dramatically reduced due to the US economic recession in 2006, and the demand for housing reduced. When demand was low, house prices reduced. As a result, an enormous number of home foreclosures occurred in 2006, and continued to grow at an uncontrolled rate in 2007. By mid-2007, mortgage issuers were overwhelmed by the number of subprime loans outstanding, leading to further foreclosures. As subprime borrowers began to default, CDO issuers were the first to collapse. Bianco (2008) stated that experts underestimated the subprime market and did not expect it to lead to vast destruction within the US economy. Twenty-five subprime lenders had declared bankruptcy in March 2007, and another 11 subprime lenders followed in April 2007.

4.3.1.3 The global financial crisis and the great recession

Apart from low interest rates, Taylor (2009) has suggested that the excessively loose monetary policy implemented by the US government may have been another contributor to the collapse of US financial institutions. The collapse of the subprime market spilled over into the US stock markets, where the Dow Jones dropped to less than 13000 (at 11346.51) and the S&P 500 went down to 1278.38 in June 2008. Subprime lenders and borrowers were badly affected, creating panic among market participants and reducing their confidence. Many interventions and measurements were implemented, including bailout packages by the US authorities, to correct the damage and increase market confidence (Furceri and Mourougane, 2009). The enormous losses were suffered directly or indirectly by the bigger US banks, leading in 2008 to the collapse of the Lehman Brothers investment bank, further verifying the fragility of the US banking system. The bankruptcy of more large US banks was subsequently announced (see Table 4.1). A low interest rate and loose financial regulation made many US banks take more leverage with the aim of achieving greater return on their investments. At the same time, the global imbalance between the saving influxes from surplus countries (China) to deficit economics (US) further worsened the global financial crisis. (Mah-Hui, 2008). Moreover, with the close integration between the economies of the US and many other countries through international trade activities, the US credit crunch contagiously affected other parts of the world (see Figure 4.2). Figure 4.2 summarizes the chronology of US housing bubble, the subprime crisis, and the 2007–2008 global financial crisis.

Table 4.1 Selected failures of financial institutions in the US and European regions in 2008

Month	*US*	*Fiscal cost*	*Europe*	*Fiscal cost*
February			UK: Northern Rock	£88 billion
March	Bear Stearns	USD 29 billion		
September	Freddy Mac and Fannie Mae	USD 200 billion	Benelux: Frotis	USB 16 billion
	Lehman Brothers	USD 639 billion	Germany: Hypo Real Estate	USD 50 billion
	AIG	USD 87 billion	Iceland: Giltnir	USD 850 million
	Wachovia (bought by Citibank)	USD 12 billion	UK: Bradford and Bingley	USD 32.5 billion
			Belgium: Dexia	USD 9.2 billion
			Ireland: Irish Bank	USD 572 billion
October			Iceland: Landsbanki, Kaupthing	USD 864 million
			Switzerland: UBS	USD 59.2 billion
			Netherlands: ING	€10 billion
			France: 6 banks	€10.5 billion
			Belgium: KBG	€3.5 billion
November			Austria: Kommunalkredit	

Source: Furceri and Mourougane (2009, p. 8)

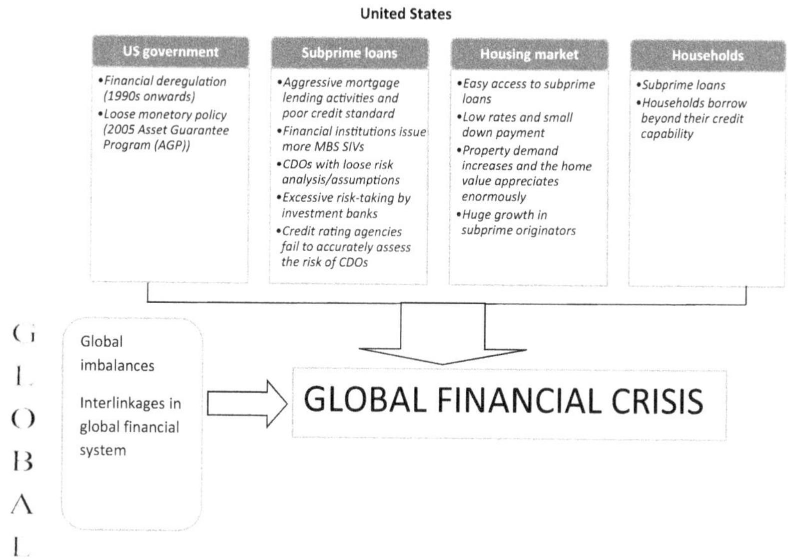

Figure 4.2 Determinants of the 2007–2008 global financial crisis

Source: Adapted from Baily, Litan and Johnson (2008); Astley et al. (2009); and Verick and Islam (2010)

This US credit crunch spilled over to the European region and further affected the European sovereign debt market in October 2008. Similar rescue packages were implemented to save European banks. Table 4.1 shows the considerable number of large European banks that were bailed out by European governments, from the UK government's rescue of Northern Rock to the Swiss government's bailout of UBS in October 2008. Due to instability in European countries, governments increased the interest rate. Standard and Poor consequently revised the sovereign debt rating of Spain, Portugal, and Greece. The American and European instability continued to spread globally, including to emerging countries. However, the effect tended to vary by emerging country – some were badly affected by the crisis while others were not.

4.3.2 US regulators' response

4.3.2.1 TARP initiatives

The global financial crisis strongly affected the financial system in the US, where it is considered more severe than the Great Depression of the 1930s. This affected the confidence level of banking institutions and resulted in a cut in lending activities. The shrinkage in credit markets providing financing to both businesses and consumers slowed down economic activity and led to further stagnation and recession in the US. This resulted in bank runs and failures in the banking and financial systems. Unemployment increased to almost 800,000 nationally losing their jobs per month and household wealth falling by 17% (US Treasury, 2016).

At the beginning of 2007, the US Treasury Department, Federal Reserve, Federal Deposit Insurance Corporation (FDIC), and other federal government agencies undertook a series of emergency actions to prevent the collapse of the US financial system. The Emergency Economic Stabilization Act (EESA) was enacted on 3 October 2008 to further rescue the financial system. EESA's objective was to stabilize and inject liquidity into the financial system in order to prevent the overall economic situation of the US from falling into stagnation. EESA gave US authorities greater flexibility in buying shares and recapitalizing banking institutions that were greatly affected during the crisis.

The Troubled Asset Relief Program (TARP) was established under EESA with the objective of restoring the country's financial stability, restarting economic growth, and preventing further banks' failures. An initial amount of USD $700 billion was authorized for the TARP in October 2008, but this was reduced to USD %475 billion by the Dodd–Frank Wall Street Reform and Consumer Protection Act (the Dodd–Frank Act). These amounts were used to set up five programs under the TARP. Details of these programs and the amounts allocated to each are presented here and in Figure 4.3:

i) Auto industry
   - to prevent the collapse of the auto industry in the US and to retain at least a million American jobs.

ii) Credit market programs
   - to restart secondary credit markets, which are crucial in boosting economic activities by maintaining credit flows to households and businesses.

iii) Invest in AIG
   - to stabilize AIG, as its failure would greatly affect the financial system and economy.

iv) Bank investment programs
   - to stabilize the banking system which was greatly affected by the financial crisis.

v) Housing
   - to prevent avoidable foreclosures and keep families in their homes.

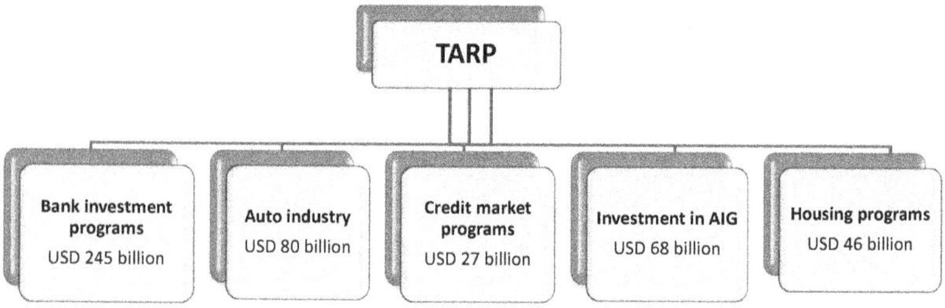

Figure 4.3 Programs under the TARP

Source: US Treasury (2016). TARP Programs. www.treasury.gov/initiatives/financial-stability/TARP-Programs/Pages/default.aspx#

The Treasury used the authority of the TARP to make investments, loans, and asset guarantees and purchases in and from a range of financial institutions with the aim of preventing further collapse of financial institutions. By doing so, the TARP encouraged banks to resume lending activities to both consumers and businesses. This was done by restoring bank capital ratios. The increase in lending activities was expected to restore the confidence of investors in financial institutions and the economy. This was expected to decrease the interbank interest rates, contributing to a lower cost of borrowing. This further boosted the lending activities and therefore contributed to better capital accumulation, helping to boost the economy.

In exchange, the Treasury, on behalf of the taxpayer, received financial instruments, including equity securities (preferred stock, common stock, and warrants), debt securities, and additional notes from these companies. The Treasury expected that the vast majority of funds disbursed through the TARP would be recovered. As of 31 October 2016, the total collections under the TARP and the non-TARP share of AIG have exceeded total disbursements by more than USD $7. 9 billion (Treasury, 2016). The Treasury thus recovered 101.8% of the USD %442 billion disbursed.

4.3.2.2 Bank investment programs

We specifically focus here on the US regulator's initiatives in the US banking industry through TARP bank investment programs. The USD $245 billion invested by the Treasury as part of the bank investment programs was not only used to rescue the large banks, but also to assist smaller banking

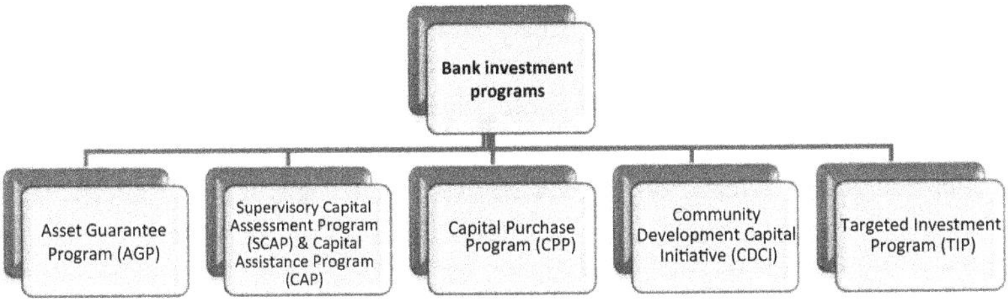

Figure 4.4 Bank investment programs

Source: US Treasury (2016). Bank investment programs. www.treasury.gov/initiatives/financial-stability/TARP-Programs/bank-investment-programs/Pages/default.aspx

institutions. This program allowed the financial institutions to sell their preferred shares to the US government. FDIC further provided a temporary guarantee of the senior debt of all FDIC-insured institutions, including holding companies. The invested funds were further segregated into five bank programs (see Figure 4.4).

4.3.2.2.1 ASSET GUARANTEE PROGRAM

The Asset Guarantee Program (AGP) was established by the US government to support banking institutions whose failure had caused serious harm to the financial system and economy. The AGP was run jointly by the Treasury, the Federal Reserve, and the FDIC to bail out banking institutions by supporting the value of certain assets held through an agreement to absorb a portion of the losses of those assets. The two banking institutions that received assistance under AGP were Bank of America and Citigroup, which had suffered from large amounts of distressed or illiquid assets during the financial crisis, resulting in the loss of market confidence. On 23 November 2007, the Federal government rescued Citigroup by absorbing losses due to toxic assets on the balance sheet and injecting fresh capital. Furthermore, on 17 January 2009, the government injected USD $20 billion into Bank of America in exchange for preferred shares, in order to absorb the losses on its balance sheet. The government also provided USD $118 billion worth of guarantees against bad assets.

Generally speaking, the AGP helped these institutions to maintain the confidence of depositors and other funding sources in order to continue meeting the credit needs of households and businesses and thus boost economic activity. At its completion, the AGP resulted in a positive return of more than USD $3 billion for taxpayers.

4.3.2.2.2 SUPERVISORY CAPITAL ASSESSMENT PROGRAM AND CAPITAL ASSISTANCE PROGRAM

The Supervisory Capital Assessment Program (SCAP) and the Capital Assistance Program (CAP) were established to ensure that the major banking institutions in the US maintained adequate capital buffers to withstand losses and to meet the credit needs of their customers in future economic recessions. This was done under the SCAP through a comprehensive stress-test that measured the health of the 19 largest bank holding companies in the US. This measure is a forward-looking test that provides unprecedented levels of transparency and clarity to the relevant authority in order to help avoid future shocks in the banking system.

Besides that, the CAP program further injected additional capital into the financial institutions that had difficulties raising capital through private sources as a result of the global financial crisis. In May 2009, the Federal Reserve report on SCAP indicated that nine out of 19 bank holding companies had sufficient capital buffers to withstand future economic shock. The CAP finished on 9 November 2009 without making any investments. Nevertheless, banks were able to raise hundreds of billions of dollars in private capital through the release of the SCAP stress-tests results.

4.3.2.2.3 CAPITAL PURCHASE PROGRAM

Capital Purchase Program (CPP) was launched to provide capital to viable financial institutions in an effort to stabilize the financial system. Under the CPP, the Treasury injected USD $205 billion into the capital positions of banking institutions. This successfully provided capital to 707 financial institutions, with the largest investment of USD $25 billion and the smallest of USD $301,000. In return, the Treasury received preferred stock or debt securities. It was reported that most financial institutions participating in the CPP paid a 5% dividend on preferred stock for the first five years, and 9% thereafter. Furthermore, the Treasury received warrants to purchase common stocks and other securities from the banks at the time of the CPP investment. This enabled taxpayers to reap additional returns on their investments, as well as assisting with the banks' recovery process.

4.3.2.2.4 THE COMMUNITY DEVELOPMENT CAPITAL INSTITUTION INITIATIVE

The Community Development Financial Institution (CDFI) was established on 3 February 2010 to provide financial services to low-income, moderate-income, minority, and other underserved communities. The CDFI banks, thrifts, and credit unions received investments of capital with an initial dividend or interest rate of 2%, as compared to the 5% rate offered under the Capital Purchase Program. The dividend rate for repayment under CDFIs was 9% after eight years, as compared to after five years under the CPP. The funding process was completed in September 2010, with total investment of about USD $570 million to 84 institutions.

4.3.2.2.5 TARGETED INVESTMENT PROGRAM

The Targeted Investment Program (TIP) was established in December 2008 to provide the Treasury with the flexibility to inject additional or new funding to financial institutions that affect the function of the overall financial system. The objective of TIP is to prevent a loss of confidence in critical financial institutions, since the failure of these institutions would affect market confidence, resulting in financial market disruptions during the crisis that would further threaten financial stability and create contagion to other financial institutions.

The Treasury invested USD $20 billion into Bank of America and Citigroup under the TIP, on top of the CPP investments these banks received. This was done through investments in preferred stock. The Treasury also received warrants to purchase common stock in each institution. The TIP investments provided annual dividends of 8%, which was higher than the CPP rate, and also imposed greater reporting requirements and more rigorous terms on the companies than the CPP.

Both companies repaid their TIP investments in December 2009, with a total of USD $3 billion dividends paid to the Treasury. The program ended with a positive return of USD $4 billion to taxpayers.

4.3.2.3 Term Auction Facility (TAF)

Aside from the TARP, the Federal Reserve also established the Term Auction Facility (TAF) in December 2007 in response to the subprime crisis and the global financial crisis. TAF enabled the Federal Reserve to provide lending to financially sound banks through US federal funds using auction windows with 28-day auctioned loans. In August 2008, the Federal Reserve also conducted an auction for 84-day loans to banks that were generally in sound financial condition. Furthermore, the Federal Reserve established a system of foreign exchange swap lines with foreign central banks. This allowed partner central banks access to dollars for lending to their own troubled banks. These two facilities enabled the Federal Reserve to create new credit by providing term funds to a broader range of counterparties, and also with a broader range of collateral, than open market operations. TAF helped to promote the distribution of liquidity when unsecured bank funding markets were under stress.

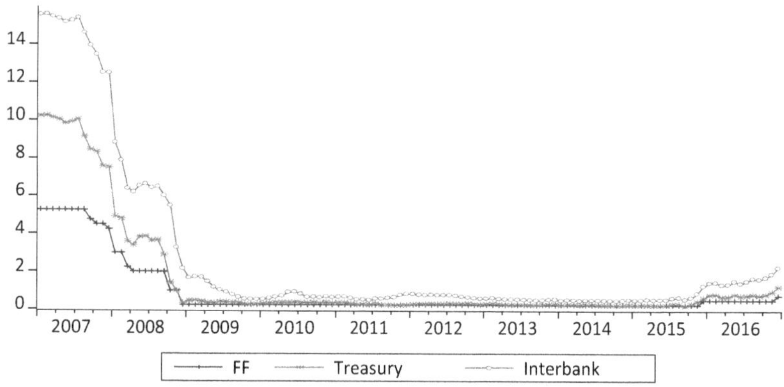

Figure 4.5 Federal Fund target rates, three-month Treasury bill, and three-month Interbank rate

Source: Thomson Datastream

4.3.2.4 Cut in Federal Fund rates

Further responding to the shrinkage in lending activities, the Federal Reserve also took the radical step of gradually cutting the Federal Fund target rates from 5.25% in August 2007 to 4.75% in September 2007. The target rate reached its lowest level of 0.25% in December 2008. This cut further led to a decrease in the three-month Treasury bill rate and the three-month interbank rate, as indicated in Figure 4.5.

The cut in Federal Fund target rates was one of the policy measures aimed at improving levels of lending activities, which had dropped off due to a lack of investor confidence in the market, affecting economic activity during the global financial crisis. This approach successfully brought the three-month Treasury bill and interbank lending rates to a low level at the end of 2008. In September 2015, the Treasury bills rate dropped to as low as -0.01%. The Federal Fund target rate began to increase, reaching 0.5% in December 2015 for the first time since 2007.

4.4 Bailout efficacy: the Malaysian and US experiences

In this section, we report on empirical studies regarding the efficacy of the bank bailouts in Malaysia and the US. The methodologies and data used are described in Chapter 2, Section 2.3.1 and Section 2.3.2.

4.4.1 The Malaysian and US bank bailout experiences

4.4.1.1 The Malaysian experience

The number of Malaysian domestic banking institutions dropped from 54 to 29 as part of the consolidation exercises under the purview of BNM. At the core of this exercise was the formation of ten banking groups leads by ten anchor banks, as described in Section 4.2.2. In fact, these merger exercises began with the finance company industry in 1998 and were soon followed by the domestic banking sector as a whole in 1999 (BNM, 1999). All of the bank institutions involved needed to choose a leader for the mergers by the end of January 2000, and the entire exercise needed to be completed by the end of December 2000.

In order to examine the performance of Malaysian commercial banks after the consolidation, we divided the overall technical efficiency of the banks into scale efficiency and pure technical efficiency. The scale efficiency shows the performance of the banks given their scale of operation. It is important to consider scale efficiency in order to determine the success of the banking consolidation, since this will determine whether the banks were able to use their resources efficiently given the increase in their scale of operation (size) after the mergers and acquisitions. On the other hand, the pure technical efficiency focuses mainly on the managerial ability to manipulate the resources of the banks to achieve a given level of outputs. In this case, the bank is said to be purely technically efficient if it is able to minimize the waste of resources so as to achieve an output level regardless of the scale of operation. Likewise, the product of scale efficiency and pure technical efficiency is the overall technical efficiency of the bank.

Table 4.2 shows the technical efficiency for Malaysian commercial banks (see also Figure 4.6). From the table and figure, we can see that banks in Malaysia enjoyed scale efficiency after the banking consolidation. The banks on average experienced higher scale efficiency of 90.9% in 2001, compared to 81.6% pure technical efficiency in the same year. This shows that the technical efficiency had its source in the scale efficiency. Nevertheless, the scale efficiency of the banks reduced from 2002, and the pure technical efficiency of the banks overtook the scale efficiency in 2003. This contributed to a reduction in overall technical efficiency from 2003. Our results are consistent with those of Matthews and Ismail (2006), who found that the scale efficiency in Malaysian commercial banks was the main contributor to the technical inefficiency. Similarly, Sufian (2010), in his analysis of the impact of the Asian financial crisis on bank efficiency in Malaysia and Thailand from 1992 to 2003, also found that the source of inefficiency lay in the scale efficiency rather than the pure technical efficiency for the Malaysian

Table 4.2 Technical efficiency score for Malaysian commercial banks

Year	*Scale efficiency*	*Pure technical efficiency*	*Overall technical efficiency*
2000	0.833	0.839	0.697
2001	0.909	0.816	0.752
2002	0.905	0.843	0.775
2003	0.836	0.901	0.758
2004	0.860	0.897	0.766
2005	0.846	0.904	0.758
2006	0.916	0.845	0.765
2007	0.857	0.882	0.760
2008	0.829	0.854	0.702
2009	0.813	0.872	0.703
2010	0.539	0.703	0.369
2011	0.534	0.720	0.355
2012	0.760	0.838	0.629
2013	0.866	0.840	0.728
2014	0.892	0.895	0.798
2015	0.795	0.813	0.639
2016	0.798	0.834	0.656

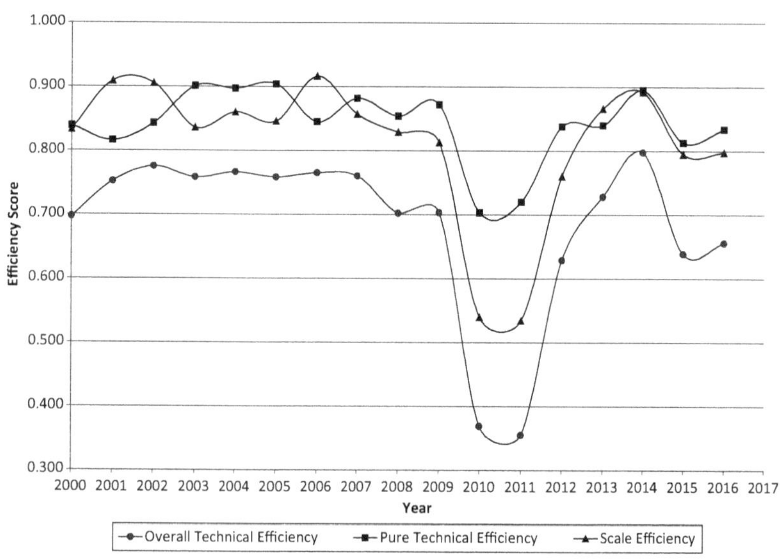

Figure 4.6 Technical efficiency scores for Malaysian commercial banks

Table 4.3 t-test for independent sample of Malaysian commercial banks

	Pure technical efficiency	*Scale efficiency*
Mean	0.838	0.805
Variance	0.045	0.049
Observations	584.000	584.000
Pooled variance	0.047	
t-statistic	2.590***	
F-test for equal variance	1.084	

Note: */**/*** denotes 10%/5%/1% significance level

banking industry. This may be because the post-merger bank industry was more concentrated and the big banks received more market power, but ultimately lost overall bank efficiency (Paul and Kourouche, 2008).

We now examine the mean differences between the pure technical and scale efficiency in order to determine whether the source of inefficiency is significant in our sample. The results of the independent sample test are shown in Table 4.3. We confirmed that scale efficiency in Malaysian commercial banks is significantly lower than pure technical efficiency. This further confirmed that the source of inefficiency of Malaysian commercial banks lies in scale efficiency.

This inefficiency may be due to the increase in the concentration ratio of the Malaysian banking industry after the consolidation, which led to the industry being dominated by ten anchor banks (refer to Figure 2.2 in Chapter 2). The number of anchor banks reduced to nine with the merger of Southern Bank Berhad and CIMB Bank Berhad in 2006. At the same time, we can observe from Figure 4.5 that the scale efficiency of commercial banks in Malaysia also began to decrease, reaching as low as 53.4% in 2011; during the same year, the number of anchor banks decreased to eight. This supports the argument put forward by Mishkin (1999), that concentrated banking industries dominated by a few larger banks are inefficient because they are more likely to receive public guarantees during bank runs. Furthermore, a concentrated banking industry leads to lower competition, which gives banks the freedom to act. Banks may take excessive risks to earn higher returns and hence become engaged in moral hazard behaviours that distort the stability of the financial system (Uhde and Heimeshoff, 2009). This position is supported by Rice and Strahan (2010), who suggest that competition is necessary to increase financial depth and promote the efficient flow of information (Claessens and Laeven, 2005), eventually reducing information asymmetry and hence enhancing the allocation of resources in the market, leading to a more stable banking system. Furthermore, concentrated banking industries result in increased market power that reduces financial soundness (Beck, Jonghe and Schepens, 2013).

As a result, we may conclude that banking consolidation needs to be carefully planned if banks are to take full advantage of economies of scale and managerial expertise. This is crucial for the long-term survivability of the banking industry in Malaysia, especially when moving towards financial integration and liberalization – which is unavoidable if the Malaysian financial system is to be brought into a higher stage of development.

4.4.1.2 The US bank bailout experience

The US bank bailout was implemented under the TARP, the largest bank bailout program in the Emergency Economic Stabilization Act of October 2008. The Capital Purchase Program (CPP) was launched specifically under the TARP with the objective of stabilizing the financial system by using higher capitalization to improve the safety and soundness of the banking industry. The implementation of the TARP led to questions of whether it was viable for the government to salvage the banking industry: such policies may result in moral hazard behaviour, because they create the perception that the banking industry will be safe during crises.

We proceed with some preliminary analysis of the bank bailout policy by analyzing the efficiency of the banking industry in the US before and after the TARP. This is done by analyzing cost efficiency, profit efficiency, and technical efficiency in the US banking industry. Table 4.4 shows the cost efficiency score for US commercial banks from 2000 to 2016.

As Table 4.4 shows, we found that commercial banks in the US were operating under cost efficiencies as low as 28.9% in 2000. This indicates that banks in the US failed to manage their cost of inputs, resulting in wastage of 71.1%. This might be because US banks were flourishing given the demand for housing loans. This is evident from Figure 4.7, which shows that the interest paid in the housing market by households in the US during 2000 was as high as 11.81%.

We similarly further see signals of bank cost inefficiency in 2007, due to the global financial crisis, where it dropped from 49.2% in 2006 to 37.6% in 2009. This was also accompanied by a large slump in the monetary interest paid by household, from 13.39% in 2006 to -7.71% in 2009, as shown in Figure 4.7.

We note that the bailout policy implemented during 2008 led to a slow increase in the cost efficiency of commercial banks in the US. The two-sample t-statistics in Table 4.5 further confirm the significant differences between the cost efficiency of commercial banks before and after the bailout.

Table 4.4 Cost efficiency score for US commercial banks

Year	*Cost efficiency*
2000	0.289
2001	0.355
2002	0.573
2003	0.344
2004	0.365
2005	0.422
2006	0.492
2007	0.485
2008	0.437
2009	0.376
2010	0.441
2011	0.457
2012	0.517
2013	0.440
2014	0.416
2015	0.504
2016	0.549

The results from the two-sample *t*-test confirm that the cost efficiency of US commercial banks increased at the 1% statistical significance level. This shows that the bailout policy significantly improved cost management of the banks.

The profit efficiency score for US commercial banks is presented in Table 4.6. Consistent with the cost efficiency, we found that their profit efficiency was as low as 55.8% in 2001 and 51.7% in 2004. This may indicate complacency on the part of the banks in utilizing their expertise for cost control and profit making, as the banks enjoyed high income due to the peak in the housing market at that time.

The two-sample *t*-test (refer to Table 4.7), assuming equal variances for profit efficiency of the US commercial banks, also confirms that the bailout policy in the US contributed to the improvement of profit efficiency after the implementation of the TARP at the end of 2008. The profit efficiency improved from 62.2% to 71.5% after the crisis, and this was statistically significant at the 1% level.

The technical efficiency scores of commercial US banks are shown in Table 4.8. Consistent with the cost and profit efficiency, we found that the overall technical efficiency of these banks was as low as 49.1% in 2000.

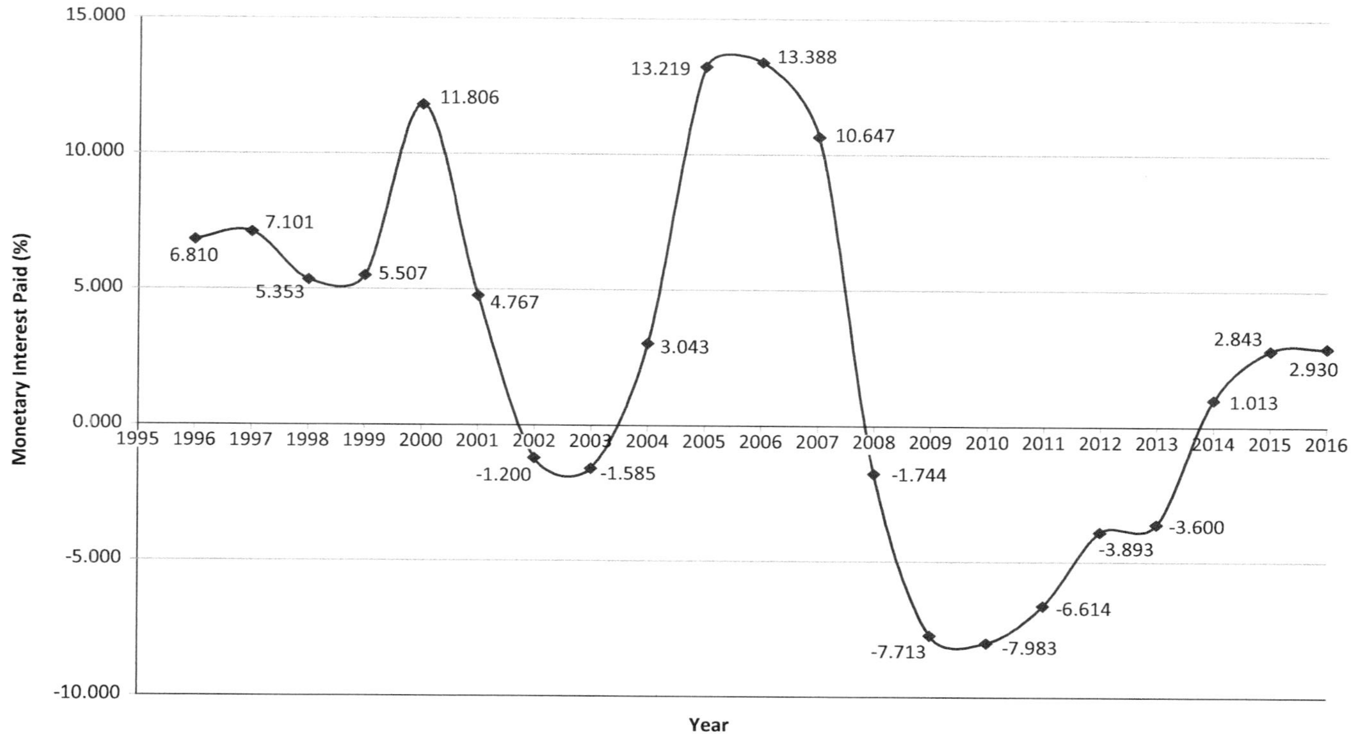

Figure 4.7 Monetary interest paid by household (year-to-year change)

Source: Bureau of Economic Analysis, US Department of Commerce

Table 4.5 Two-sample t-test assuming equal variances for cost efficiency for US commercial banks

	Before crisis	*After crisis*
Mean	0.399	0.458
Variance	0.095	0.099
Observations	466	347
t-statistic	–2.690***	
F-statistic for equal variances	1.051	

Note: */**/*** denotes 10%/5%/1% significance level

Table 4.6 Profit efficiency scores for US commercial banks

Year	*Profit efficiency*
2000	0.570
2001	0.558
2002	0.704
2003	0.607
2004	0.517
2005	0.714
2006	0.736
2007	0.708
2008	0.813
2009	0.792
2010	0.622
2011	0.744
2012	0.601
2013	0.664
2014	0.733
2015	0.676
2016	0.803

Table 4.7 Two-sample t-test assuming equal variances for profit efficiency for US commercial banks

	Before crisis	*After crisis*
Mean	0.622	0.715
Variance	0.109	0.094
Observations	466	347
t-statistic	–4.137***	
F-statistic for equal variances	1.159*	

Note:*/**/*** denotes to 10%/ 5%/1% significance level

Table 4.8 Technical efficiency score for US commercial banks

Year	*Scale efficiency*	*Pure technical efficiency*	*Overall technical efficiency*
2000	0.735	0.669	0.491
2001	0.684	0.681	0.476
2002	0.805	0.788	0.639
2003	0.746	0.752	0.557
2004	0.741	0.702	0.526
2005	0.784	0.797	0.635
2006	0.828	0.835	0.698
2007	0.852	0.784	0.676
2008	0.905	0.879	0.796
2009	0.899	0.851	0.764
2010	0.737	0.753	0.555
2011	0.917	0.794	0.729
2012	0.856	0.741	0.623
2013	0.839	0.783	0.655
2014	0.811	0.791	0.643
2015	0.764	0.808	0.621
2016	0.782	0.907	0.712

This indicates that the banks were wasting an average of 50.9% of their inputs in the production of financial products and services. Decomposing the efficiency scores into scale efficiency and pure technical efficiency shows that the source of inefficiency lies in the pure technical efficiency. The banks' managements are unable to manage the allocation of resources, resulting in wastage of inputs in the production process. This again demonstrates the complacency of management in working with the bank's resources while the institutions are enjoying high incomes from the peak in the housing market.

The bank bailout significantly improved the technical efficiency of commercial banks in the US. We note that both the scale and pure technical efficiency of the commercial banks improved after the global financial crisis. Use of an ANOVA test (see Table 4.9) further confirms the significant improvement in banking practices in the US after the bailout. Results of the Tukey–Kramer test further confirm that the efficiency scores are different for all sub periods, and this shows that the efficiency of US banks improved significantly after the global financial crisis.

Table 4.9 Comparison analysis of US banks' technical efficiency scores

Groups	*Count*	*Sum*	*Average*	*Variance*	F-*test*
Overall technical efficiency					
Before crisis	421	231.803	0.551	0.077	30.328***
During crisis	167	122.149	0.731	0.053	
After crisis	225	145.302	0.646	0.068	
Pure technical efficiency					
Before crisis	421	306.865	0.729	0.059	14.780***
During crisis	167	139.637	0.836	0.036	
After crisis	225	178.098	0.792	0.052	
Scale efficiency					
Before crisis	421	314.727	0.748	0.052	22.532***
During crisis	167	145.116	0.869	0.023	
After crisis	225	183.854	0.817	0.042	

Note: */**/*** denotes 10%/5%/1% significance level

References

Allen, F., and Gale, D. (2000). *Comparing Financial Systems*. Cambridge, UK: MIT Press.

Allen, F., and Gale, D. (2004). Competition and financial stability. *Journal of Money, Credit, and Banking*, *36*(3), 453–480.

Amidu, M., and Wolfe, S. (2013). Does bank competition and diversification lead to greater stability? Evidence from emerging markets. *Review of Development Finance*, *3*, 152–166.

Astley, M.S., Giese, J., Hume, M.J., and Kubelec, C. (2009). Global imbalances and the financial crisis. *Bank of England Quarter Bulletin, 2009 Q3*, 177–190.

Baily, M.N., Litan, R.E., and Johnson, M.S. (2008, November). The origins of the financial crisis. *Initiative on Business and Public Policy at Brookings, Fixing Financial Series*, Paper 3, 1–47.

Bank Negara Malaysia (1999). *The Central Bank and the Financial System in Malaysia: A Decade of Change (1989–1999)*. Kuala Lumpur: Bank Negara Malaysia.

Bank Negara Malaysia Annual Report 1999. Retrieved from http://www.bnm.gov.my/index.php?ch=en_publication&pg=en_ar&ac=3&lang=en

Beck, T., Jonghe, O.D., and Schepens, G. (2013). Bank competition and stability: Cross-country heterogeneity. *Journal of Financial Intermediation*, *22*, 218–244.

Berger, A.N., Klapper, L.F., and Turk-Ariss, R. (2009). Bank competition and financial stability. *Journal of Financial Services Research*, *35*, 99–118.

Bianco, K.M. (2008). *The Subprime Lending Crisis: Causes and Effects of the Mortgage Meltdown*. New York: CCH, Wolters Kluwer Law & Business.
Boot, A.W.A., and Greenbaum, S. (1993). Bank regulation, reputation and rents: Theory and policy implications. In C. Mayer and X. Vives (Eds.), *Capital Markets and Financial Intermediation* (pp. 262–285). Cambridge, UK: Cambridge University Press.
Boot, A.W.A., and Thakor, A.V. (2000). Can relationship lending survive competition? *Journal of Finance*, *55*, 679–713.
Boyd, J.H., and De Nicolo, G. (2005). The theory of bank risk-taking and competition revisited. *Journal of Finance*, *60*, 1329–1343.
Boyd, J.H., De Nicolo, G., and Jalal, A. (2009). Bank risk-taking and competition revisited: New theory and evidence. Working Paper WP/09/143 IMF. Retrieved from https://www.imf.org/en/Publications/WP/Issues/2016/12/31/Bank-Competition-Risk-and-Asset-Allocations-23047
Boyd, J.H., De Nicolo, G., and Smith, B.D. (2004). Crisis in competitive versus monopolistic banking systems. *Journal of Money, Credit and Banking*, *36*, 487–506.
Boyd, J.H., and Prescott, E.C. (1986). Financial intermediary-coalitions. *Journal of Economic Theory*, *38*, 211–232.
Boyd, J.H., and Runkle, D.E. (1993). Size and performance of banking firms: Testing the predictions of theory. *Journal of Monetary Economics*, *31*, 47–67.
Brunnermeier, M.K., Dong, G., and Palia, D. (2011). Banks' non-interest income and systemic risk. Working Paper, Princeton University and Rutgers University.
Caminal, R., and Matutes, C. (2002). Market power and bank failures. *Journal of Industrial Organisation*, *20*, 1341–1361.
Carletti, E., Hartmann, P., and Spangnolo, G., (2007). Bank mergers, competition, and liquidity. *Journal of Money, Credit, and Banking*, *36*, 1067–1105.
Cetorelli, N., and Peretto, P.F. (2000). Oligopoly banking and capital accumulation. Working Paper, No. 2000–2, Federal Reserve Bank of Chicago.
Claessens, S., and Laeven, L. (2005). Financial dependence, banking sector competition and economic growth. *Journal of the European Economic Association*, *3*, 179–207.
Craig, B., and Santos, J. (1997). The risk effect of bank acquisitions. *Federal Research Bank of Cleveland Economic Review*, *QII*, 25–35.
Crotty, J. (2009). Structural causes of the global financial crisis: A critical assessment of the 'new financial architecture'. *Cambridge Journal of Economics*, *33*(4), 563–580.
Danaharta. (2006). *Financial Report 1998–2005*. Pengurusan Danaharta National, Kuala Lumpur.
D'Arista, J., and Griffith-Jones, S. (1998). The boom of portfolio flows to emerging markets and its regulatory implications. In S. Griffith-Jones, M.F. Montes, and A. Nasution (Eds.), *Short Term Capital Flows and Economic Crises* (pp. 52–69). Oxford, UK: Oxford University Press.

Das, D.K. (1999). *Asian Economic and Financial Crises: Causes, Ramifications and Lessons* (pp. 1–22). Canberra: Asia Pacific School of Economics and Management, Asia Pacific Press.

Demsetz, R., Saidenberg, M.R., and Strahan, P.E. (1996, October). Banks with something to lose: The disciplinary role of franchise value. *Economic Policy Review*. Federal Reserve Bank of New York, 1–14.

De Nicolo, G., and Loukoianova, E. (2007). Bank ownership, market structure and risk. IMF Working Paper No. 07/215, 1–46.

Diamond, D. (1984). Financial intermediation and delegated monitoring. *Review of Economic Studies*, *51*, 393–414.

Eichengreen, B., and Mussa, M. (1998). *Capital Account Liberalization: Theoretical and Practical Aspects*. Washington, DC: International Monetary Fund.

Furceri, D., and Mourougane, A. (2009). Financial crises: Past lessons and policy implications. OECD Economic Department Working Papers, 668. Paris: OECD Publishing.

Hannan, T.H., and Prager, R.A. (1998). The relaxation of entry barriers in the banking industry: An empirical investigation. *Journal of Financial Services Research*, *14*, 171–188.

Hellmann, T.F., Murdock, K.C., and Stiglitz, J.E. (2000). Liberalization, moral hazard in banking, and prudential regulation: Are capital requirements enough? *The American Economic Review*, *90*(1), 147–165.

Holt, J. (2009). A summary of the primary causes of the housing bubble and the resulting credit crisis: A non-technical paper. *Journal of Business Inquiry*, *8*(1), 120–129.

IMF. (1998). *World Economic Outlook*. Washington, DC: International Monetary Fund.

IMF. (1999a). *Malaysia: Selected Issues*. Washington, DC: International Monetary Fund.

IMF. (1999b). *World Economic Outlook*. Washington, DC: International Monetary Fund.

Jiménez, G., Lopez, J.A., and Saurina, J. (2013). How does competition affect bank risk-taking? *Journal of Financial Stability*, *9*, 185–195.

Kaminsky, G.L., and Schmukler, S.L. (2008). Short-run pain, long-run gain: Financial liberalization and stock market cycles. *Review of Finance*, 253–292.

Kaplan, E., and Rodrik, D. (2001). *Did the Malaysian Capital Controls Work? National Bureau of Economic Research*, 1–49.

Keeley, M.C. (1990). Deposit insurance, risk, and market power in banking. *American Economic Review*, *80*(5), 1183–1220.

Koskela, E., and Stenbacka, R. (2000). Is there a tradeoff between bank competition and financial fragility? *Journal of Banking and Finance*, *24*(12), 1853–1873.

Mah-Hui, M.L. (2008). Old wine in new bottles: Subprime mortgage crisis: Causes and consequences. *Journal of Applied Research in Accounting and Finance*, *1*(1), 3–12.

Marcus, A.J. (1984). Deregulation and bank financial policy. *Journal of Banking and Finance*, *8*(4), 557–565.

Martinez-Miera, D., and Repullo, R. (2010). Does competition reduce the risk of bank failure? *Review of Financial Studies, 23*(10), 3638–3664.

Matthews, K., and Ismail, M. (2006). Efficiency and productivity growth of domestic and foreign commercial banks in Malaysia. *Cardiff Economics Working Papers*, No. E2006/2, 1–23.

Mayer, C.J., and Pence, K. (2008). Subprime mortgages: What, where, and to whom? No. w14083, 1–41, National Bureau of Economic Research.

Mirzaei, A., Moore, T., and Liu, G. (2013). Does market structure matter on banks' profitability and stability? Emerging vs. advanced economies. *Journal of Banking and Finance, 37*, 2920–2937.

Mishkin, F.S. (1999). Financial consolidation: Dangers and opportunities. *Journal of Banking and Finance, 23*, 675–691.

Paroush, J. (1995). The effect of merger and acquisition activity on the safety and soundness of a banking system. *Review of Industrial Organization, 10*, 53–67.

Paul, S., and Kourouche, K. (2008). Regulatory policy and the efficiency of the banking sector in Australia. *Australian Economic Review, 41*(3), 260–271.

Radelet, S., and Sachs, J. (1998). *The Onset of the East Asian Financial Crisis*. Cambridge, UK: National Bureau of Economic Research.

Rice, T., and Strahan, P.E. (2010). Does credit competition affect small-firm finance? *Journal of Finance, 65*(3), 861–889.

Saunders, A., and Wilson, B. (1996). Bank capital structure: Charter value and diversification effects. Working Paper Series, 96–52, Salomon Center, New York University.

Schaeck, K., and Cihak, M. (2012). Banking competition and capital ratios. *European Financial Management, 18*(5), 836–866.

Schaeck, K., Cihak, M., and Wolfe, S. (2009). Are competitive banking systems more stable? *Journal of Money, Credit, Banking, 41*(4), 711–734.

Shaffer, S. (1998). The winner's curse in banking. *Journal of Financial Intermediation, 7*, 359–392.

Stiglitz, J. (2002). *Globalization and Its Discontent*. London: Penguin.

Sufian, F. (2010). Does foreign presence foster Islamic banks' performance? Empirical evidence from Malaysia. *Journal of Islamic Accounting and Business Research, 1*(2), 128–147.

Taylor, J.B. (2009). The financial crisis and the policy responses: An empirical analysis of what went wrong. No. w14631, National Bureau of Economic Research.

Uhde, A., and Heimeshoff, U. (2009). Consolidation in banking and financial stability in Europe: Empirical evidence. *Journal of Banking and Finance, 33*(7), 1299–1311.

Verick, S., and Islam, I. (2010). The great recession of 2008–2009: Causes, consequences and policy responses. No. 4934, 1–61.

Vives, X. (2011). Competition and stability in banking. In L.F. Céspedes, R. Chang, and D. Saravia (Eds.), *Monetary Policy under Financial Turbulence* (pp. 455–502). Central Banking, Analysis and Economic Policies Book Series. Santiago: Central Bank of Chile.

Wang, J. (2007). Financial liberalization and regulation in East Asia: Lessons from financial crises and the Chinese experience of controlled liberalization. *Journal of World Trade*, 211.

Williamson, S. (1986). Costly monitoring financial intermediation, and equilibrium credit rationing. *Journal of Monetary Economics*, *18*, 159–179.

World Bank. (1998). *East Asia: The Road to Recovery*. Washington, DC: The World Bank.

5 Conclusion

Rozaimah Zainudin and Chan Sok-Gee

This book has provided useful insights into Malaysian banking practices since the 1997 Asian financial crisis (AFC). We have discussed the policies and practices of banking in Malaysia after the AFC by first evaluating the overall health of the industry in Malaysia through bank efficiency analyses and, second, examining the risk management evolution and practices of Malaysian banks after the AFC and the global financial crisis (GFC), in response to the International Basel Capital Accords I, II, and III, as well as the policy changes implemented by BNM and future challenges. Third, the book has examined the effectiveness of bank bailouts in Malaysia by comparing bailout policies with those of banking sectors in developed countries.

The Data Envelopment Analysis (DEA) was used to measure overall bank health in Malaysia. DEA is a nonparametric approach to evaluating bank efficiency. In this context, the analysis was in terms of profit, cost, and technical efficiency of the banks and aimed to provide a comprehensive study of banking operations and practices, not only from the profit generation point of view, but also with respect to cost control and the management of the bank resources. The results suggest that strict credit selection among banks and the economic slowdown further affected the demand for financial products and services during the GFC period, which translated into the low profit efficiency experienced by Malaysian banks in 2008. The cost efficiency of banks however deteriorated from the time of the AFC to 2016, perhaps due to the increase in the price of banks' production factors that pressure banks to absorb the rising cost and cause them to inefficiently allocate resources. The implementation of the Goods and Services Tax (GST) in 2015 may have exerted further cost pressure on banks. The extreme deterioration in overall cost efficiency was however due to Islamic banks' worse performance, rather than that of the conventional banks. However, a more stable technical efficiency was seen among Malaysian commercial banks, indicating that these held stable in resource allocation after the pricing of inputs and outputs has been factored out. Overall, the focus of Malaysian policy makers and bank management – especially in Islamic banks – was on improving bank cost efficiency so as to remain competitive and stable and absorb any excessive external pressure.

Various policies had been implemented and improved from the bank risk management perspective, to create a more resilient and stronger banking industry that can respond to unexpected external shocks. BNM has continued to adopt various measurements for the banking sector in tandem with the International Basel committee standards – namely Basel I in 1989, Basel II in 2005, and Basel III in 2016 – to allow more accurate bank risk exposure. The chapter further evaluates the best practices among leading world banks in the US, UK, and China in terms of five aspects of best practice that cover capital adequacy, asset quality, earnings and profitability, liquidity, and sensitivity of financial institutions to market risk – which is emphasized by the International Monetary Fund's Financial Soundness Indicators. These indicators show that Chinese banks have outstanding performance compared to the banks of other mature economies, such as the US and UK, especially in terms of earning ability and asset quality; this is surprising, as Chinese banks are dominated by state-owned banks. ICBC Bank, the largest bank in the world in recent years, was found to be superior in generating higher earnings and profitability and maintaining asset quality, and tends to be less volatile in response to market risk than banks in developed economies. Surprisingly, Malaysian banks are considered superior to US banks in capital adequacy, asset quality, and liquidity. This may due to the prudential measures that have been put into place since the AFC. Based on these indicators, Malaysian bank loans were more concentrated in certain industries; hence, to reduce exposure, these banks need to diversify their loan concentration distribution. Once this is done, the unsystematic risk derived from a specific industry will be lessened.

When comparing the performance of leading banks in the UK (Royal Bank of Scotland), US (Citigroup), China (Industrial and Commercial Bank of China), and Malaysia (Malayan Banking Bhd), we found that the Industrial and Commercial Bank of China was the top performer in terms of profitability, and had lower credit risk during the GFC period than Royal Bank of Scotland and Citigroup. In addition, the largest bank in Malaysia (Malayan Banking Bhd) fell behind, especially in terms of return on equity, compared to the world's largest banks. Malayan Banking Berhad also tended to have a lower efficiency ratio. This evidence suggests that Malayan Banking Bhd needs to enhance the allocation efficiency of its assets to avoid excessive expenses and allow it to become competitive in the world. The future challenges to Malaysian banks include the changing landscape of bank consumers, competitive operating costs, and the era of fintech.

Finally, this book has compared the effectiveness of the bailout and merger strategies applied to Malaysian banks and to US banks during the AFC and the GFC periods, respectively. The effectiveness of the merger and bank bailout strategies was assessed by comparing the technical efficiency frontier (scale efficiency and pure technical efficiency). In the Malaysian bank merger exercise, we found that the scale efficiency in commercial banks was significantly lower than the pure technical efficiency, implying that scale efficiency is the source of the inefficiency in Malaysian commercial banks. Based on this statistical evidence, the bank merger exercises following the AFC period were unable to increase the scale efficiency. The Malaysian policy makers need to reconsider merger strategies on Malaysian banks in the future, since it may not guarantee that overall bank performance improves as a result of taking full advantage from economies of scale and managerial expertise. This is crucial for the long-term survivability of the banking industry in Malaysia, especially when moving towards financial integration and liberalization – which is unavoidable if the authorities plan to bring the Malaysian financial system into a higher stage of development.

Regarding the US bank bailout experience during the GFC period, we first measured the US bank efficiency in terms of profit, cost, and technical aspects. Overall, the results suggest that commercial banks in the US operate with low cost efficiency and fail to manage the costs of their inputs effectively, resulting in the wastage of more than half of their resources. As for profit efficiency, those US commercial banks that benefitted from the GFC bailout policy and TARP were able to improve their overall profit efficiency at the end of 2008. In contrast with Malaysian banks, the source of overall technical inefficiency among the US banks was pure technical efficiency, rather than scale technical efficiency. Pure technical inefficiency refers to an inability on the part of banks to allocate banking resources to produce financial services and products, which may be due to the mismanagement of bank resources before the crisis or the drop in lending during the GFC period. This means that the banks were faced with an inability to allocate resources correctly, which resulted in the wastage of inputs during the production process. This again points to the complacency of bank management in dealing with banking resources while they were enjoying high income from the peak in the housing market. Overall, the bank bailout strategy was able to improve the total technical efficiency of US banks, unlike Malaysian banks. Since the GFC period, the results have suggested that US banks' technical efficiency underwent a significant improvement.

6 Special topic

Practitioner insight on risk management practices[1]

Eric H. Y. Koh[2]

6.0 Introduction

This chapter has three aims: first, it traces the evolution of the risk management function in Malaysian banks. Second, it outlines some key best practices observed in two leading global banks. Third, it discusses the main future challenges confronting risk management professionals. Despite the increasing importance of risk management in banks, there seems to be a dearth of publications on the developments in risk management among Malaysian banks. For instance, the last known authoritative book on the topic was published by Malaysia's central bank, Bank Negara Malaysia, some two decades ago in 1999 under the title The Central Bank and the Financial System in Malaysia: A Decade of Change 1989–1999. Among its key foci is banking sector regulation during the Asian financial crisis.

Most publications on banking in Malaysia cover specific aspects, but are not comprehensive. For instance, Powell (2017) compares bank risk in Malaysia to that in ASEAN, using measures such as impaired loans, conditional distance to default, and tail risk. Shuhidan, Hamidi and Saleh (2017) examine how young Malaysian adults perceive the risks inherent in mobile banking. Further, while AuYong (2014) attempts to bridge the divide between theory and practice, he focuses on the disclosure of current practices under the categories of credit, market, operational, and liquidity risks. The foregoing discussion suggests that these publications focus on specific bank risk aspects in Malaysia; however, they do not discuss some key milestones in the industry, or what to expect next.

This chapter attempts to fill this gap. It is organized as follows: Section 6.1 traces the evolution of the risk management function by studying developments in the risk-related regulatory aspects. It then reviews the banks' annual reports for risk-related themes and developments. Section 6.2 reviews the annual reports of two banks that are global leaders in risk management. This review provides the basis for identifying some key best practices that Malaysian banks could consider adapting. Section 6.3 reviews pertinent works of leading global consultants to gauge the potential future challenges confronting risk management professionals.

This section examines how the risk management function has evolved at Malaysian banks. It also discusses how the risk-related standards and guidelines of Bank Negara Malaysia (the Malaysian central bank) have evolved and influenced the development of banks' risk management functions.

6.1 The evolution of risk management in Malaysian banks

Before delving into these matters, however, we take a look at Kloman (2010), who provides a good overview of the evolution of risk management. This overview facilitates further understanding and analysis. In the earliest of times, human beings survived through the genetic expression of leveraging their experience and minds to reduce uncertainties in obtaining the essentials of food, warmth, and protection. The next phase was to attribute good and bad favour to divine creatures. Over time, people came to believe that they could think intelligently about the future, because they began to believe that they are, to some extent, in control of their destinies. They also became more interested in numbers and probabilities, and hence began exploring future possibilities by scrutinizing the past. This led to a shift from seeing risk as an unavoidable fate to a more scientific study of possible outcomes, probabilities, and choices. This scientific approach forms the theoretical foundation for risk management today.

Kloman (2010) also mentions the formation of three major professional bodies in risk management: the Risk Management Association (RMA) in 1914, the Global Association of Risk Professionals (GARP) in 1996, and the Professional Risk Managers' International Association (PRMIA) in 2000. RMA traces its roots to Robert Morris Associates, which was named after Robert Morris, who helped establish the American banking system (Risk Management Association, 2018). RMA initially focused on credit risk – very much a reflection of the fact that its founders were American credit and lending officers. However, RMA today, much like GARP and PRMIA, promotes an "enterprise approach" that extends beyond credit risk to other risk categories, such as market, operational, and securities lending risk and regulatory issues (Risk Management Association, 2018). The evolution of risk management of banks globally (Malaysia included) very much mirrors RMA's shift from credit risk to a more enterprise-focused approach. In 1992, GE Capital's James Lam became the first person to use the title "Chief Risk Officer" (CRO) (Kloman, 2010). Despite being relatively new (spanning less than three decades), "risk management has become more recognized as a professional discipline" (Lam, 2014, p. 342).

6.1.1 Items studied

In order to study how the risk management function has evolved over time, we set up a spreadsheet with years as category headers and risk-related items as content, similar to Babbie (2010, p. 407). We also adapted the content analysis approach of Karanja and Rosso (2017), who analyzed banks' press releases to identify how the Chief Risk Officer's roles and responsibilities fit into Mintzberg's classical managerial roles model. More specifically, we apply Hsieh and Shannon's (2005) summary of content analysis. We analyze pertinent keywords – namely "risk," "Chief Risk Officer," and "enterprise-wide risk management" or "integrated risk management" – in Malaysian banks' annual reports. This facilitates an understanding of the context and underlying meanings of the content pertinent to the evolution of the risk management function. Further, in order to obtain a better background perspective, we also review pertinent publications on developments in the risk management function, the Chief Risk Officer's roles, and Bank Negara Malaysia's (BNM) website.

6.1.2 The regulatory landscape

We review the "standards and guidelines" section of BNM's website to search for items which substantially discuss "risk" and/or "risk management". Table 6.1 shows the pertinent risk-related standards and guidelines.

A review of Table 6.1 suggests a few findings: first, unlike in earlier years, when BNM issued one risk-related standard and guideline annually, more recent years have more. The years 2013 to 2015 see three risk-related documents issued annually. In the two subsequent years of 2016 and 2017, this increased to eight and ten, respectively.

Second, the standards and guidelines issued in earlier years pertained mainly to credit risk and Basel regulatory capital requirements. These were, and still are, very much the bread and butter or core requirements for banks. The standard entitled Best Practices for Credit Risk Management was issued in 2001. This standard marks an important milestone as BNM intensified its efforts to strengthen the banks' credit risk management infrastructure and underwriting practices in the aftermath of the 1998 Asian financial crisis (AuYong, 2014). It is the start of, among other things, the requirement for bank personnel handling credit risk matters to be professionally certified. It also calls for an independent credit risk management function. It is only 17 years later, in 2018, that a new Credit Risk standard replaces the original version. The more scientific and rigorous requirements of Basel II

Table 6.1 Risk-related standards and guidelines issued by BNM

Year	*Number issued*	*Title*
2001	1	Best Practices for Credit Risk Management (superseded by "Credit Risk" Jan 2018)
2005	1	Guidelines on Investment Banks
2007	1	Guidelines on Data Management and Management Information System (MIS) Framework
2008	1	Prudential Standards on Securitization Transactions
2010	1	Risk-Weighted Capital Adequacy Framework (Basel II): Disclosure Requirements (Pillar 3)
2011	1	Notification on the Implementation of Basel III
2012	1	Risk-Weighted Capital Adequacy Framework (Basel 1: Risk-Weighted Assets Computation)
2013	5	Guidelines on Investment in Shares, Interest-in-Shares, and Collective Investment Schemes
		Risk-Weighted Capital Adequacy Framework (Basel II): Internal Capital Adequacy Assessment Process (Pillar 2)
		Risk Governance
		Fit and Proper Criteria
		Risk-Informed Pricing
2014	3	Introduction of New Products
		Single Counterparty Exposure Limit
		Guidelines on Credit Transactions and Exposures with Connected Parties
2015	3	Classification and Impairment Provision for Loans/ Financing
		Requirements for the Conduct of Money Services Business by Banking Institutions
		Repurchase Agreement Transactions
2016	8	Statutory Reserve Requirement
		Compliance
		Operational Risk
		Corporate Governance
		Reference Rate Framework
		Shareholder Suitability
		Liquidity Coverage Ratio
		Financial Technology Regulatory Sandbox Framework

Table 6.1 (Continued)

Year	*Number issued*	*Title*
2017	10	*Credit Risk: Exposure Draft (UPDATED TO Credit Risk_ Jan2018_PD 029–22)*
		Capital Adequacy Framework (Basel II: Risk-Weighted Assets)
		Regulated Short-Selling of Securities in the Wholesale Money Market
		Stress-Testing
		Exposure Draft on Net Stable Funding Ratio
		Exposure Draft on Outsourcing
		Principles for a Fair and Effective Financial Market for the Malaysian Financial Market
		Management of Customer Information and Permitted Disclosure
		Leverage Ratio
		Observation Period Reporting (Capital Adequacy Ratios, Liquidity Coverage Ratio, and Leverage Ratio)

(subsequently mandated by BNM) saw more intense expectations from BNM and greater investment by banks in systems and methodologies.

Third, the Risk Governance document issued in March 2013 effectively pools together other guidelines into a "complete and cohesive risk management framework," which includes the "creation of a Chief Risk Officer (CRO) role" (AuYong, 2014). Unlike the traditional banking practice of equating risk management with credit risk management, the CRO also oversees other risk categories, such as market, operational, and liquidity risks. It also marks yet another important milestone in fostering a risk-aware culture in banks by calling for a dedicated risk management function and setting stringent requirements for the CRO. This shift is in line with our earlier discussion of the evolution of professional bodies such as RMA from a credit risk focus to an enterprise approach to risk.

For instance, clause 42 of Risk Governance says that the CRO must have

> good knowledge of the business and the relevant qualifications, technical skills and experience in risk disciplines to enable him to lead the effective implementation of the risk management framework . . . have strong communication skills to be able to effectively engage the board on risk matters and constructively interact with the CEO and other senior management on risks affecting the financial institution.
>
> (Bank Negara Malaysia, 2013)

This long list of idealistic requirements expected of a CRO seems similar to the three broad roles of chief compliance officer, business partner, and strategic advisor (Karanja and Rosso, The Chief Risk Officer: a study of roles and responsibilities, 2017). Such high expectations regarding CROs' qualifications are needed to ensure that the bank complies with Principle 7 of Risk Governance – that is, that the risk management function must have "sufficient authority, stature, independence, resources, and access to the board" (Bank Negara Malaysia, 2013). Put another way, a strong and respected risk management function is needed to "rectify a critical imbalance of power – with the back office control functions . . . dominated by front office trading and investment functions" (Lim et al., 2017, p. 1).

Fourth, 2016 sees the departure of the earlier emphasis on credit risk in favour of a more comprehensive CRO perspective of risk. These newer standards and guidelines extend to other risk categories, such as liquidity risk and operational risk. They also extend to other risk-related areas, such as compliance and corporate governance. Moreover, in line with developments beyond the traditional banking activities, these standards and guidelines also govern newer, rapidly developing areas, such as financial technology (fintech) and outsourcing.

In sum, BNM's risk-related standards and guidelines have increased not only in number, but also in their scope and sophistication, in step with current banking industry developments. While some banks may have already adopted these requirements before these documents were issued, others are now required to follow suit.

6.1.3 Developments in banks' risk management practices

A review of risk-related matters in the Malaysian banks' annual reports suggests that the two largest banks, Maybank and CIMB, disclose more than the others in terms of the level of detail and number of initiatives. This may be due to their more intense, complex, and sophisticated risk management development, brought about by their larger pool of resources and necessitated by their much larger scale and complexity of business activities.

In terms of the pertinent keywords, Figure 6.1 shows how many times the word "risk" appears in each bank's annual reports over the years.

A review of Figure 6.1 suggests that, in general, all banks show an increasing trend. The trend reflects the escalating importance and complexity of risk management due to Basel compliance requirements and increasing regulatory pressure to strengthen banks' resilience since the global financial crisis (Bessis, 2015). Indeed, the Malaysian banks' annual reports devote more space to discussing regular matters, such as the yearly progression of Basel II adoption, the composition of risk-related committees, work done, and further risk management refinements and initiatives. The disclosures also

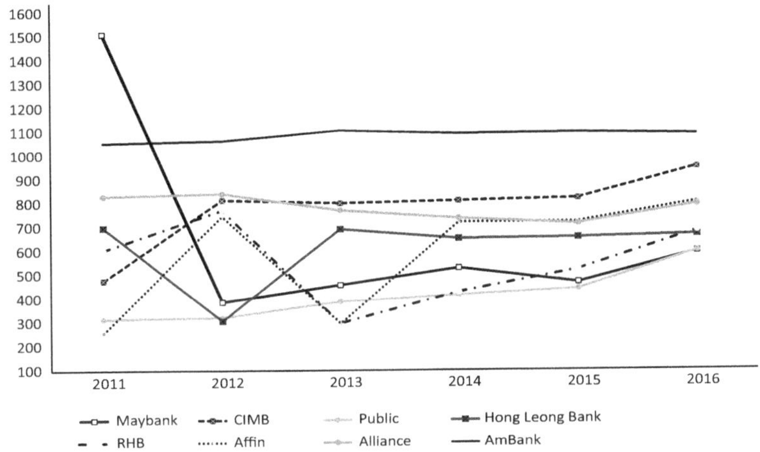

Figure 6.1 Number of times "risk" appears in annual reports

extend to the more distant future, such as assessment of potential Basel III implications and the use of advanced risk and big data analytics.

Maybank's reports show a spike in the occurrence of the word "risk" in 2011, before hitting more normal levels from 2012 on. The spike in 2011 perhaps coincides with the ex-KPMG Partner Dr John Lee's joining as the bank's new CRO. In 2011, Maybank disclosed its longer term vision of "fully integrating risk as a key driver of risk return optimization focused on value creation and active portfolio management" (Maybank, 2011, p. 234). It also celebrated its success in migrating to the Basel II internal ratings-based approach for credit risk to compute risk-weighted assets, and extensively discussed its various risk mitigation strategies across risk categories. Further, Maybank also disclosed for the first time its Basel II Pillar 3 market disclosure requirements. Another strategic initiative which Maybank revealed was its "comprehensive risk talent management blueprint to . . . articulate core risk competencies. . . . In addition, [Maybank] defined the training curriculum to build the required risk capabilities . . . and succession planning" (Maybank, 2012, p. 4).

Next, enterprise-wide (or integrated) risk management is a new holistic paradigm in managing risk (Togok, Isa and Zainuddin, 2016). Unlike previous approaches that handle risks in silos, enterprise-wide risk management sees all risk areas as working components of an integrated overall system, in which top management provides oversight and all employees "view risk management as an integral and ongoing part of their jobs" (Fraser and Simkins, 2010, p. 3). A formal definition of enterprise-wide risk management has been provided by the Committee of Sponsoring Organizations of the Treadway Commission (COSO):

> Enterprise risk management deals with risks and opportunities affecting value creation or preservation . . . [it] is a process, effected by an entity's board of directors, management, and other personnel, applied in strategy setting and across the enterprise, designed to identify potential events that may affect the entity, and manage risk to be within its risk appetite, to provide reasonable assurance regarding the achievement of entity objectives.
>
> (COSO, 2004, p. 2)

In 2017, COSO issued its Updated Framework, which gives more insights into how enterprise risk management adds value to the strategy setting and implementation process. It also more clearly links enterprise risk management with various stakeholder expectations, places risk as an integral rather than separate part of a firm's performance, and facilitates more proactive risk anticipation so as to enhance value and not merely minimize losses (COSO, 2017). Meanwhile, another key industry-sanctioned model is the International Organization for Standardization's (ISO) 31000:2009. This ISO model defines risk management as the "coordinated activities to direct and control an organisation with regard to risk" and the enterprise risk management framework is woven into the firm's "overall strategic and operational policies and practices" (Karanja, 2017, p. 280). In 2018, ISO's revised standard "provides more strategic guidance . . . and [emphasizes] . . . the involvement of senior management and the integration of risk management into the [firm]" (ISO, 2018, p. 3).

In terms of implementing enterprise-wide or integrated risk management, a review of the annual reports suggest that Maybank and Hong Leong Bank led the way in 2001, followed by CIMB in 2003, Public Bank, and RHB Bank in 2004, Alliance Bank in 2005, Ambank in 2006, and Affin Bank in 2008. Maybank's genesis to enterprise-wide risk management began with the need to integrate its key risk categories into an integrated framework accountable to the Board's Risk Management Committee, so as to enhance overall risk management (Maybank, 2001). In 2002, Mr Choo Yee Kwan was appointed the first CRO of Maybank, and probably of any Malaysian bank (Maybank, 2002). Meanwhile, Hong Leong Bank's journey began with the setting up of a new Integrated Risk Management division to oversee bank-wide risks in preparation for the new Basel Capital Accord (Hong Leong Bank, 2002). It is not clear who Hong Leong Bank appointed as its first CRO, or when this happened.

Implementing enterprise-wide risk management is both challenging and important, as banks strive to capture, measure, and report risks across all business functions, product lines, customers, and risk categories in a consistent, comprehensive, integrated manner. The enterprise-wide or integrated risk management framework provides the Board of Directors and top management with a standardized approach to managing current and potential changing risk profiles. Its typical key components are governance and organization, risk appetite, risk management process (business planning, risk identification, measure and assess, manage and control, monitor, and report), supported by risk management infrastructure (of policies, procedures, and methodologies, people, technology, and data) and risk culture (CIMB, 2016). While risk culture is broadly defined as one in which the bank's staff take cognizance of risks and strive to optimize the bank's risk–return trade-off, Public Bank's list perhaps makes this more explicit. The pertinent items are "strong corporate governance, organizational structure with clearly defined roles and responsibilities, effective communication and training, commitment to compliance with laws, regulations, and internal controls, integrity in fiduciary responsibilities, clear policies, procedures, and guidelines" (Public Bank, 2013, p. 112).

6.1.4 Summary

In summary, risk management traces its roots to a time when people went beyond leaving outcomes to fate, and began to more rigorously examine probabilities and outcomes. It has also moved beyond a credit risk focus to an enterprise approach. Today, risk management takes a more holistic view by considering the key risk categories, such as market, operational, and liquidity risks. The regulatory landscape has intensified as the central bank has issued an increasing number of standards and guidelines aimed at elevating risk management professionalism and banking sector resilience. In response, Malaysian banks have stepped up their risk management initiatives beyond the routine compliance and Basel matters to more forward-looking plans. The Basel II requirements saw the banks investing heavily in systems and methodologies to more rigorously quantify risks. Malaysian banks have also moved to enterprise-wide or integrated risk management.

6.2 Global best practices: a preliminary study of two leading banks

This section aims to give a preliminary view over some of the best practices adopted by two banks regarded by the industry as among the best in risk management. We begin by discussing the choice of these banks, followed by the methodology, and finishing with an outline of the key best practices.

6.2.1 Why JPMorgan Chase and Deutsche Bank?

We have selected JPMorgan Chase (JPMC) and Deutsche Bank (DB) for the following reasons: JPMC has long been regarded as a leader in enterprise-wide risk management, as it has strong risk management functions and its leaders appreciate and manage risks well. In fact, its Chairman and CEO Jamie Dimon is sometimes dubbed "the chief risk officer" (Kaplan and Mikes, 2012; Lam, 2014). JPMC first developed RiskMetrics, the "de facto benchmark for market risk" (Lam, 2014, p. 347) and also paved the way for credit derivatives. But unlike other bankers, who were blinded by the prospects of extraordinary profits, JPMC exited the market when it could not gauge the default correlation just before the 2008 global financial crisis (Flood, 2009). A reputable risk magazine, Risk.net, also named JPMC the bank risk manager of the year in 2012 (Risk.net, 2012).

We selected DB because Risk.net named it the bank risk manager of the year in 2011, 2014, and 2015. Moreover, Global Finance has consistently ranked DB as among the 25 safest banks in the world, at least from 2015 to 2017 (Global Finance, 2015, 2016; Cunningham, 2017).

At the same time, we note that these two banks have also shown weaknesses. For instance, JPMC paid a hefty fine of at least USD $13 billion for mishandling mortgages and also suffered an infamous USD $6 billion derivatives trading loss (Koh, Avvari and Tan, 2016). DB, on the other hand, has been fined USD $70 million for alleged manipulation of an interest rate derivatives benchmark (Scheer, 2018), was fined USD $630 million for alleged failure to prevent Russian money laundering, and paid a USD $7.2 billion settlement for a toxic bond mis-selling scandal (Treanor, 2017).

Nonetheless, no bank is perfect. All have had their share of blunders and brushes with various regulatory authorities. Taken in context, we seek to identify some best practices of JPMC and DB, two global banks that have relatively better track records for their strength in risk management.

6.2.2 Items studied

In line with this section's aims, we review three years of these banks' recent annual reports. The review seeks to identify their key discussions on risk management matters and its developments over the three financial years of 2014, 2015, and 2016. We also refer to the banks' investor relations pages and other pertinent external resources that can shed light on these best practices.

6.2.3 Findings

A review of the three recent annual reports suggests that both JPMC and DB emphasize two items – namely, conduct risk and derisking. The other key items seen are JPMC's fortress principle, frequent stress-tests, rigorous model risk and development, security analytics, a cross-business focus on asset-deposit strategy groups, and industry specialists. DB also seems to stand out on its handling of forward-looking macroeconomic forecasting and compensation matters.

6.2.3.1 Key items in both JPMC and DB

Conduct risk, a new and emerging risk category, has attracted attention in the light of scandals and penalties that have hit many leading global banks as a result of activities such as mis-selling and trading misconduct. This refers to the chance that the staff breach standards of professionalism, ethics, or laws which may adversely impact clients, the firm's reputation, financial market integrity, or even disrupt the regulator's competitive agenda (Imeson, 2015; Financial Conduct Authority, 2018). The importance of conduct risk is exemplified by JPMC's appointment of a Chief Culture and Conduct Officer, the establishment of a separate risk category for Conduct Risk in 2016, and the development of a culture and conduct risk dashboard that is reviewed with the Board of Directors and senior management (JPMorgan Chase & Co., 2017a). Likewise, in 2014, DB set up a Conduct and Control Group, added 700 people to the control units within the business functions, and sent some 6000 people to dedicated compliance and risk culture workshops (Deutsche Bank, 2015).

Figure 6.2 shows the key best practices adopted by JPMC and DB.

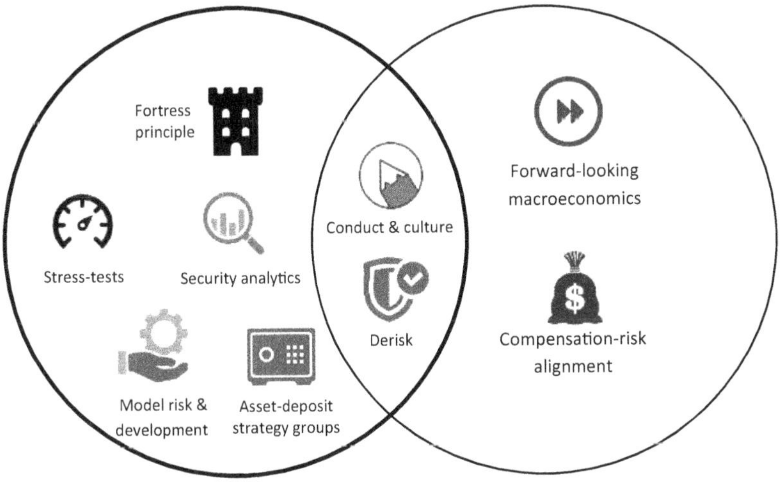

Figure 6.2 Key best practices of JPMC and DB

Conduct risk arises when banks, which are inundated with huge volumes of data and process automation, fail to identify the behavioural aspects that are the real underlying root causes of problems in their risk assessments (Engler, 2017). Besides launching a firm-wide culture and conduct program in 2014 to strengthen its behavioural principles, JPMC has also established a "culture and conduct risk assessment and dashboard" to manage conduct risks (JPMorgan Chase & Co., 2017b). Examples include having an algorithm that monitors emails to identify potential bad behaviour (Clarke, 2015), excessive trading transaction cancellations or corrections, and breaching compliance requirements of mandatory block leave (Engler, 2016).

The second item that features at both banks is derisking. This entails exiting from transactions or customer relationships which are too complex, risky (be it in terms of credit, legal, regulatory, or political aspects), or attract potentially undesirable reputational ramifications. JPMC hired a team in 2014 for this task and has exited relationships with some 8,000 wholesale business customers, 5,500 foreign politically exposed persons, and 500 foreign correspondent banks (JPMorgan Chase & Co., 2015, 2016). Meanwhile, DB relies on its noncore operations unit to reduce the risks inherent in its noncore assets, liabilities, and businesses. DB has also restricted complex derivatives deals to selected customer segments, worked on resolving outstanding litigation matters, and strengthened new customer intake screening procedures (Deutsche Bank, 2015, 2016, 2017).

6.2.3.2 Key items at JPMC

This subsection discusses five key items observed in a review of JPMC's annual reports. First, in its statement on business principles, JPMC lays claim to its concept of an "unquestionably strong" or "fortress balance sheet," which emphasizes strength in capital, liquidity, reserves, and risk discipline to enable the bank to weather economic storms. This also calls for, among other things, a thorough understanding of its balance sheet, assigning accountability and having strong controls (JPMorgan Chase & Co., 2017c). In recent years, JPMC has also added specialized bankers and underwriters in key industries (e.g., healthcare, agriculture, and technology), expanded its data analytics/intelligence capabilities, and further invested to strengthen its "fortress risk and compliance framework" (JPMorgan Chase & Co., 2015, 2016, 2017c).

Second, JPMC prides itself in having intense stress-tests, doubling from 100 per week in 2014 and 2015, to 200 in 2016 (JPMorgan Chase & Co., 2015, 2016, 2017a). These tests are conducted worldwide and analyzed in various ways to ensure that the bank can survive many extreme scenarios. Third, JPMC's model risk and development exercises are also rigorous, as they involve more than 300 employees who have completed more than

500 model reviews and have implemented a system to evaluate the performance of the most complex models (JPMorgan Chase & Co., 2005).

Fourth, JPMC's investments in security analytics technology include those for big data in risk management, so as to combat fraud, detect employee fraud and bad behaviour, and use web browser isolation technology to mitigate the risk of employees being compromised through phishing. Fifth, JPMC has brought together the Asset Strategy group and Deposit Strategy group to facilitate cross-business deliberations on lending, investments, and deposits so as to assess related risks (JPMorgan Chase & Co., 2017a).

6.2.3.3 Key items at DB

This subsection discusses two key items at DB. First, DB has incorporated forward-looking macroeconomic factors since 2017 so as to assess risks and measure IFRS9-compliant expected credit loss. This is also used as the basis for conducting DB's capital planning and stress-testing (Deutsche Bank, 2017). Second, DB checks whether its compensation plans and performance evaluation systems are appropriately aligned to its risk appetite. This is deliberated by the Compensation Control Committee. This committee, together with the Risk Committee, evaluates the effects of its compensation systems on the bank's risk, capital, and liquidity conditions (Deutsche Bank, 2015, 2017).

6.2.4 Summary

We selected two banks reputed to be among the best in risk management practices globally – JPMorgan Chase and Deutsche Bank. While it may be worth considering adapting their best practices, we must note that they have also committed significant mistakes, too. Their key best practices noted here include enhancing conduct and culture, derisking, adopting the fortress balance sheet concept, intensifying stress-tests, improving security analytics, facilitating cross-functional asset and deposit-strategy group discussions, incorporating forward-looking macroeconomic indicators in risk models, and improving the risk–reward link.

6.3 Future challenges

This section aims to study the potential challenges that may face the risk management function of banks in future. In light of the growing complexity and global interconnectedness of banking activities, the risk management function will be confronted with even more intense and varied challenges. We infer these future challenges mainly from a study of pertinent publications by leading global consultants that have reported the findings of their surveys, interviews, and discussions, as shown in Table 6.2.

Table 6.2 Key publications: leading consultants' studies, coverage, and method

Author/firm	*Location*	*Aspects/ industries*	*Methods*
Accenture (2015a)	Global	risk; capital markets	• Surveyed 470 senior risk management executives. • Interviewed senior leaders from 50 leading organizations. • Talked to 170 capital markets executives.
Accenture (2015b)	North America	risk; banks, capital markets and insurance	• Surveyed 150 respondents in the North American banking, capital markets, and insurance firms (offshoot of Accenture, 2015a).
Deloitte (2013)	Americas, Europe/Middle East/Africa, and Asia/Pacific	strategic risk; five key industries including financial services	• Surveyed over 300 respondents, predominantly C-level executives, board members, and specialized risk executives. • Interviewed executives of eight leading firms.
Deloitte University Press (2017)	Global	risk; financial services	• Surveyed 77 firms.
Friedman (2016)/ Deloitte	US	cyber-risk; financial services	• Interviewed Chief Information Security Officers (CISOs) and cyber-risk management professionals.
Härle et al. (2015)/McKinsey	Global	risk; banks	• Talked to senior executives, CROs, and senior risk managers.
Ivell and Jain (2014)/Oliver Wyman	Global	operational risk; financial services vs. capital-intensive industries	• Surveyed 27 firms across financial services and capital-intensive industries.
Jackson (2015)/ EY	Global	risk; banks	• Surveyed top banks by asset size in each region (51 banks, 29 countries). • Interviewed CROs and senior risk executives.
Lascelles and Patel (2015)/PwC	UK, US, and Europe	risk; banks	• Surveyed 672 bankers, risk managers and regulators, and close observers of banks in 52 countries.

Table 6.3 Key publications: leading consultants' knowledge bases

Author/firm	*Location*	*Aspects/industries*
Bector et al. (2015)/Oliver Wyman	Global	cyber-risk; key industries
Daisley, Howard-Jones and Naylor (2014)/Oliver Wyman	Global	risk; incentives
Deloitte (2016)	UK	information technology (IT) risks; financial services
EY (2014)	Global	risk; banks
Hida and Leake (2017)/ Deloitte	US, Australia, Luxembourg, Canada	risk; financial services
PwC (2015a)	UK	cyber-risk
PwC (2015b)	Global	model risk; financial services
Stylianides, Dawson and Moseley (2015) (PwC)	UK	risk; financial services
Waslo et al. (2017)/Deloitte	US	cyber-risk

Besides, observations from these firms' knowledge base – although not obtained from customized surveys – were also studied (see Table 6.3).

These publications provide a good knowledge base for discussions of the future challenges that confronting the risk management function of banks. This section, however, attempts to analyze, infer from, and organize the various insights obtained into a more comprehensive and overarching framework which comprises the four categories of regulation, technology, emerging risks, and competencies, as shown in Figure 6.3.

6.3.1 Regulation

The earlier trend towards deregulation, driven by the call for greater efficiency, seems to have reversed since the 2008 global financial crisis. The eruption of the crisis caught many by surprise and the extent of damage it caused was the greatest since the 1930s Great Depression. The trend since the crisis seems to be towards reregulation, as authorities tighten and introduce new measures to control the adverse effects of the crisis and to rebuild the public's confidence in financial systems. Moreover, the regulatory authorities are intent on preventing a similar crisis very soon after the 2008 phenomenon. Indeed, the flurry of activity around increased regulation has caused "many CROs [to] worry they are being pulled more and more into the role of 'Chief Regulations Officer' [rather than] devoting attention to risks as they affect the business" (Jackson, 2015, p. 4). So much time and effort is

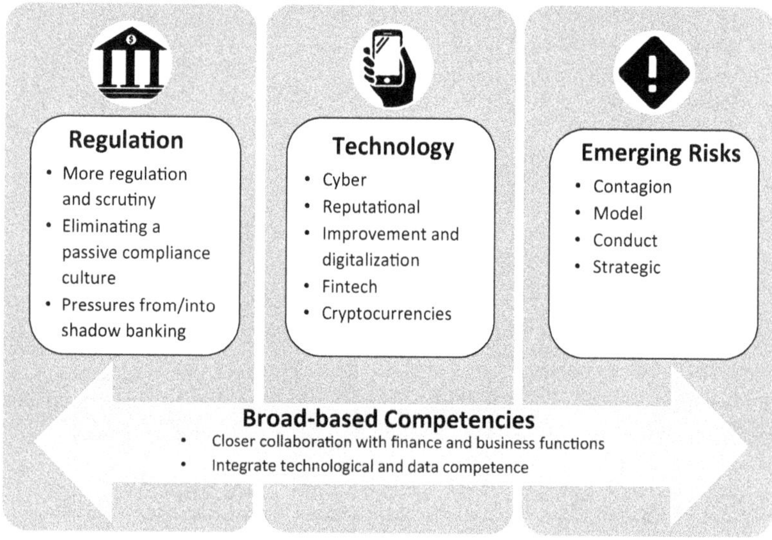

Figure 6.3 Future challenges for risk management

expended on compiling, extracting, and manually adjusting data merely to satisfy regulatory requirements to the extent that the true focus and added value that a CRO brings to the business is being questioned. Besides this question, the risk management function must also grapple with increased cost pressures to possess the requisite data technology infrastructure, burdensome work for its staff, and a shortage of talent (Härle et al., 2015).

Regulatory-related pressures are likely to increase, and manifest themselves in at least three forms. First, there will be even more regulatory spotlight on banks, especially on the risk management function. Not only will the current stringent requirements continue, but the regulators will step up pace in imposing new regulations and scrutinizing banks even more closely (Ernst and Young, 2014). This is due in part to the increasingly risky environments in a more globally interconnected world. Banks have also been severely fined for their deficiencies in financial crime compliance. The increased prevalence of financial crime, exacerbated by technological sophistication and increased transaction volumes, will render financial crime compliance even more challenging and its budgetary needs seemingly unending. As such, some have called for a collaborative industry-wide utility approach to address this matter (Meurant, 2014). Yet the move towards reregulation is also triggered by apparent bank weaknesses. It is not only the apparently weaker or smaller banks that are cracking under pressure. In fact, even once-revered leading global banks are being heavily penalized, are failing stress-tests, and are forced to adjust their capital plans (Accenture, 2015b).

Second, in light of the overwhelming regulatory pressures, banks seem to have become more passive, at least in operational risk management, as compared with other capital-intensive industries such as energy, aviation, and natural resources (Ivell and Jain, 2014). Both banks and these capital-intensive industries have been exposed to major operational losses. This includes rogue trading in banks, energy plant accidents, aviation accidents, and oil spills. Banks, however, seem to lag behind these other industries in terms of their operational risk response capability.

The pressures to cope with increased banking regulatory demands perhaps drive banks' risk management functions towards a quasi-robotic mode, rather than towards one which proactively reflects and manages risks more strategically, as was originally intended. In order to break away from this passive compliance culture and to move towards one that is more proactive, banks need to reduce internal finger-pointing and curb excessive but unclear preventative controls. Instead, banks should learn from these other industries by exploring ways to encourage discussions and to share lessons learnt in a way that respects a risk-aware culture and promotes transparency (Ivell and Jain, 2014; Lascelles and Patel, 2015).

Third, a potentially darker side effect of over-regulation is the rise of "shadow banks," which are not under the purview of the banking regulators. Such shadow banks are nonbanks that offer bank-type services and which are subject to less regulation. The lighter regulations imposed on such firms pose a strategic risk to banks, because it threatens the important mediation role of the banks (Lascelles and Patel, 2015). Moreover, if the unregulated shadow banking sector continues to grow, more financial activities will move towards this sector, increasing systemic risks. Should this happen, increased regulations would ironically produce the opposite of what the regulators originally intended. In fact, "many . . . remain skeptical" as to whether increased rules and regulations will be able "to change the corporate culture [of large complex banks' excessive risk-taking] that caused the 2008 financial crash" (Lam, 2014, p. 291). Perhaps, banks would do well to strengthen their risk management, both in substance and form, so as to provide confidence to the regulators of the banks' soundness and hence, to facilitate dialogue aimed at agreeing to a more sustainable rate of regulation.

In summary, while regulations are needed to control bank risks, over-regulation may divert the CRO's attention away from his or her core focus areas. Banks expend significant time, effort, and cost on coping with the regulatory pressures. Besides, banks can expect to face even more new regulations and scrutiny from regulatory authorities. In fact, the over-regulation of banks has caused banks to become more passive and to lag behind other industries in managing operational risks. Finally, shadow banks may pose a strategic risk to banks, and may also raise systemic risks in the financial system as they operate in a less regulated regime.

6.3.2 Technology

Besides regulation, technological matters are also often cited as key challenges for the risk management function in future. The breakneck pace of technological advancement serves is both a bane and a boon to the risk management function. On the one hand, banks are exposed to more risks, which appear and multiply at an increasingly rapid pace. On the other hand, the risk management function has opportunities to enhance its efficiency and effectiveness. There at least three key technology-related challenges: cyber-risks, reputational risks arising from increased use of social media, and digitalization.

One of the biggest challenges is the increasing risk of cyber-security (Accenture, 2015a; Härle et al., 2015; Deloitte University Press, 2017). It is, in fact, among the ten risks "most likely to cause a global crisis" (Bector et al., 2015, p. 13). Cyber-security risk relates to the chances that a bank may suffer losses caused by "attacks on operating systems; locking users out of their computers and data; theft or corruption of data and systems; and release of confidential data, intellectual property, or corporate strategy" (Deloitte University Press, 2017, p. 13). This will inevitably increase with increased reliance on "software, systems, information technology (IT), and data" (Härle et al., 2015, p. 13), together with internet-based interfaces. Banks, however, find it a challenge to employ the right talent to maintain pace with the ever-changing, fast-moving target of increasing cyber-security threats.

While there is increasing demand from various stakeholders for improved cyber-security, the lack of industry benchmarks makes it hard for cyber-risk professionals to measure their banks' state of cyber-security maturity. Indeed, the search for appropriate cyber-risk metrics (that are understandable, common across the banking sector, and automatable) is challenging (Friedman, 2016).

The increasing prevalence of cyber-security warrants its treatment as a permanent risk to the entire firm that should be treated as a business imperative, rather than as an isolated information technology event (Bector et al., 2015; PwC, 2015a). Much like the other established risk categories of credit, market, and operational risks, the business functions should also own the first line of defence against cyber-risk – something which CROs have not been able to instil. In fact, a bank's risk-awareness culture should be extended to include a cyber-risk aware culture element which could be facilitated and enhanced by a Cyber-Risk Operations team and a Cyber-Risk Management Committee (PwC, 2015a).

Cyber-security is not merely about the bank's internet interface. Banks also need to study their digital supply chain, as data is increasingly shared (Waslo et al., 2017). Banks need a more integrated approach to protecting their systems, data, and connected devices. Cyber-security must be built into the design processes throughout the supply chain. Besides, with the increasing complexity and prevalence of cyber-risks, banks may also employ robotics and artificial intelligence mechanisms to help detect threats from both transactional and cyber-risks (Accenture, 2015a). However, putting it all together in place will need a blend of more expertise in technology management, security, fraud, and cyber-risks (Deloitte, 2016).

Another consequence of increased internet connectivity is the rise of reputational risk stemming from heightened social media exposure (Deloitte, 2013; Accenture, 2015a). News, real or otherwise, travels much faster and can easily turn viral through social media. While banks can use social media for marketing and promotional activities, they must be increasingly vigilant of the potentially higher reputational risks arising from unfavourable comments on social media, such as Facebook, YouTube, and Twitter.

On the positive side, the risk management function can use technology to enhance its efficiency and effectiveness. It can employ tools such as natural language generation, machine learning, cognitive intelligence, and crowdsourcing so as to further automate the risk reporting processes and to enhance early risk detection and the sourcing of ideas (Hida and Leake, 2017; Accenture, 2015a; Härle et al., 2015). Technology can also provide near real-time data to facilitate decision-making and analytics to facilitate better projections (Accenture, 2015b). In fact, the risk management function should minimize manual intervention and obtain one set of consistent data in its report generation tasks. Yet it will find itself under more pressure to minimize headcount growth, so it will be necessary to automate tasks as much as possible in order to focus on the crucial and complex risk matters (Härle et al., 2015). In other words, banks need to have a digital risk transformation program (Portilla et al., 2017). Such a program requires significant effort and bank-wide support. The key requirements include data management, process, and workflow automation, advanced analytics and decision automation, good infrastructure, smart visualization and interfaces, an external ecosystem (i.e., partnerships with established peers, utilities, and start-up firms), and talent and culture. This comes with a cost, the justification for which may be challenging in times of uncertainty for the banking industry.

Third, financial technology (fintech) is a fast growing area. As fintech developments are fluid, their impact on banks remains uncertain. Nonetheless, the risk of fintech disruption may have wide-ranging repercussions in the areas of "strategic risk, operational risk, cyber-risk and compliance risk" (Basel Committee on Banking Supervision, 2017, p. 2). Finally, one uncertain area of development is that of cryptocurrency. On one hand, because of its virtual nature, cryptocurrency may facilitate an "Internet of Value" that enables one to be one's own market maker anywhere and to trigger transactions quickly at virtually no cost (Undheim, 2014, p. 2). On the other hand, there may be higher risks of money laundering as it is harder to trace funds in cryptocurrency systems (BAE Systems, 2016). Further, cryptocurrency may disrupt banking business to the extent of eliminating the bank's traditional intermediary role in the payment system.

In summary, fast changing technological developments present at least three implications. First, cyber-risks will increase in line with the banks' increased dependency on systems, technology, and data. Second, reputational risks arising from increased use of social media will need to be even better managed. Third, the risk management function should also make use of technology to enhance its effectiveness and efficiency through digitalizing risk.

6.3.3 Emerging risks

Emerging and new risks may surface from time to time. While it is impossible to provide an exhaustive list of these, those discussed more often include contagion, model, conduct, and strategic risks. First, the impact of contagion risks is increasingly widespread and intense because of increasing "financial and macroeconomic interconnectedness" (Härle et al., 2015, p. 13). Risk models are often not sufficiently robust to incorporate such risks because they are built largely on the basis of historical experience and normal expectations. The challenge is that people tend to forget major shocks and extreme and outlying events, such as the global financial crisis, which may invalidate the models. It is thus important to regularly conduct stress-tests on models and to check for parameter and variable updates. Stress-tests should include reverse stress-tests in order to ascertain adverse scenarios that could threaten a bank's viability. Starting with the known adverse outcome, reverse stress-tests facilitate the identification of possible various future scenarios and "uncover hidden risks and interactions among risks" (Basel Committee on Banking Supervision, 2009, p. 14; Bank Negara Malaysia, 2017). Further, the risk management function should strive to reduce judgement biases by using analytics or algorithms in machine learning, facilitating constructive debates, and setting up organizational measures such as qualitative credit assessments (Härle et al., 2015).

Second, as banks rely increasingly on quantitative risk models, the risks arising from model deficiencies – referred to as model risk – will also increase. Deficiencies may arise from weaknesses in data quality, conceptual soundness and implementation, or unexpected major departures in correlation and volatility patterns (Härle et al., 2015). In order to mitigate this risk, banks need to increase rigour in the model development phase, obtain better-quality data over a longer time horizon, and improve the implementation and monitoring processes. PriceWaterhouseCoopers (PwC) hypothesizes that banks typically employ fairly rigorous processes during the model development phase, while the ongoing model monitoring process may be insufficient in terms of "frequency, scope, and breadth of testing" (PwC, 2015b, p. 3). PwC's proposed continuous model monitoring (CMM) process seeks to proactively manage a model's performance by having an independent team track model performance on daily, systematic, and consolidated bases vis-à-vis predetermined metrics. The CMM process may also facilitate earlier identification, and hence earlier warning, of emerging risks.

The third category of emerging risk is conduct risk, which is "a top issue because of the range of adverse events . . . and the huge cost to the industry from a variety of conduct and compliance events" (Jackson, 2015, p. 19). Conduct risk refers to chances of financial or reputational damage caused by employee misconduct in the form of unethical behaviour – such as mis-selling products, money laundering, market abuse, and unauthorized trading (Jackson, 2015; Lascelles and Patel, 2015). Despite heavy penalties and tighter controls, such risks will persist because of human weakness and temptation. Nonetheless, mitigation measures can be taken. Some banks, upon identifying such risks in their current business approach, decide to drop products or withdraw from some markets, change incentives, change sales targets, and clearly move risk accountability to the front office. Banks also need to step up their efforts to measure conduct risk and increase accountability for conduct risk in the business functions. This may take the form of running risk control self-assessments and enterprise governance, risk, and compliance tools to track or reduce the chances of misconduct incidences. In fact, technological tools – such as robotics, automation, and data analytics – may help reduce the chances of misconduct by reducing manual interventions and identifying staff behavioural and communication patterns. There is indeed an increasing need for the implementation of a firm-wide formal and systematic conduct and culture program (Hida and Leake, 2017).

The fourth category is strategic risk items, which are those that "affect or are created by [a bank's] business strategy and strategic objectives" (Deloitte, 2013, p. 3). Strategic risk becomes more prominent because of uncertainties and volatilities arising from challenges and changes in geopolitics, regulation, and technology disrupters, such as fintech start-ups (Jackson, 2015; Hida and Leake, 2017) and other niche players like the Apple Pay payment system (Accenture, 2015b). Strategic risks should even include nonquantifiable items, such that banks should also integrate qualitative soft data (e.g., regulation or reputation) to provide a more comprehensive view of the real risks they are facing (Deloitte, 2013). Studying strategic risks can also be viewed as pulling together the discussions in the preceding subsections on regulation, technology, and emerging risks; it can be seen as top-down or macro view that serves to complement or even crosscheck the bottom-up view of the three risk items discussed earlier.

In summary, emerging or new risks can be expected to manifest from time to time. Although it is impossible to present an exhaustive list of such items, the risk management function needs to be alert to such possibilities. This subsection has discussed the four major emerging risk items – namely contagion, model, conduct, and strategic risks.

6.3.4 Competencies

To recapitulate, the discussions in the preceding three subsections on future challenges in the areas of regulation, technology, and emerging risks suggest that the risk management function of the future will need to be competent in at least the following:

i) proactively managing risk by discussing and reflecting on lessons learnt;
ii) identifying the potential risks triggered by technological developments and trends;
iii) using technology to enhance risk-related efficiency and effectiveness;
iv) running stress-tests to gauge the potential impact of contagion risks;
v) developing risk models and undertaking continuous monitoring;
vi) facilitating conduct and culture programs.

These competency requirements converge on the theme of integration, in that the risk management function cannot work in isolation but must increasingly engage other functions effectively and integrate pertinent broad-based competencies. This may be challenging, even as the risk management function has itself "only recently started to manage risk in an integrated fashion" (Lam, 2014, pp. 289–290). In other words, even as the risk management function is stepping up its integrated risk management efforts, it will also need to quickly integrate other pertinent competencies.

Besides integrating technological and data competence, the risk management function will also need to integrate well with the finance and business functions. The risk and finance functions share similar challenges, as they both need to address the regulators' increasing demands and scrutiny in a cost-effective way, to seek to enhance data quality and consistency, to simplify processes, to articulate key messages (despite being confronted with more complexities), and to add value by providing better business insights (Accenture, 2015a). Examples of such applications include the internal capital adequacy assessment process (ICAAP) mandated by the Basel Accord and the increasing emphasis on better risk appetite determination since the global financial crisis (KPMG, 2013).

The risk management function also needs to collaborate even more closely with the business functions to enhance information connectivity and to meet the higher expectations of directors, leadership, and business functions (Ernst and Young, 2014). In fact, the risk management function needs to speak not just about controlling risk: the progressive risk management function of the future needs to work closely in partnership with the business function in the areas of business strategy and growth, so that it considers the risk – return trade-off and becomes a key growth enabler (Accenture, 2015a; Stylianides, Dawson and Moseley, 2015). This would also facilitate a more connected view of risks across businesses and instil a more consistent risk culture bank-wide. This is because the understanding of risk culture is typically in silos that are not consistent across the different functions of a bank, on account of job functions, geographic diversity, and resistance from the business function. Closer collaboration and engagement would help reduce these inconsistencies and resistance. Moreover, such close collaboration would also facilitate more career path opportunities via more flexible cross-functional staff movements in the face of talent shortage (Daisley, Howard-Jones and Naylor, 2014).

6.3.5 Summary

In the fast changing world of banking and finance, there are many challenges that will confront risk management professionals. While there are endless permutations and combinations of these items, the challenges may be broadly categorized as intensifying regulatory pressures, technological disruptions, and emerging risks while building a broader-based comprehensive range of competencies.

6.4 Conclusion

This chapter set out to trace the evolution of risk management in Malaysian banks, to identify key best practices in the approach to risk management adopted by leading global banks, and to discuss the potential future challenges confronting risk management professionals. There are four key findings: first, the number of risk-related standards and guidelines issued by the central bank has increased exponentially. This provides guidance and impetus for continued development in risk management, and also enhances the resilience of banks. Second, Malaysian banks have also shown tremendous progress in risk management, with all of them stating that they have already implemented enterprise-wide risk management. Third, some best practices adopted by two leading global banks, JPMorgan Chase and Deutsche Bank, may be considered for adoption in Malaysia. The key items include reinforcing good conduct and culture and derisking as appropriate. Items for consideration based on JPMorgan Chase's practices include adopting the fortress balance sheet concept, intensifying stress-tests, improving security analytics, and facilitating cross-functional discussions, such as among the asset and deposit-strategy groups. Meanwhile, items for consideration based on Deutsche Bank's practices include the incorporation of forward-looking macroeconomic indicators and improving the link between risks and rewards. Third, the key challenges that will confront risk management professionals in the future may be seen in areas of intensifying regulation, rapid technological development, emergence of other risk items, and the need for broader-based competencies.

These findings present three implications: first, they contribute to knowledge in an important but under-researched area – namely developments in risk management among Malaysian banks. They shed some light on the key milestones in both the regulatory landscape and on the practices adopted by banks. Second, policy makers may wish to consider reviewing current regulatory requirements and policies with a view to a more resilient banking system, though one that is not overly burdened with regulatory compliance matters. Third, practitioners may wish to reflect on past developments, to consider potential learning points from two leading global banks, and to prepare for the challenges ahead.

While this chapter attempts to contribute to the important area of risk management development in Malaysia, it is not without its limitations. Perhaps the key limitation lies in the methodology. This chapter's findings are based mainly on reviews of the Malaysian bank's annual reports, the central bank's standards and guidelines, and other pertinent publications. In order to shed more light on the findings, future researchers may wish to consider conducting interviews, focus groups, or surveys to triangulate and strengthen the body of evidence and knowledge obtained. This limitation, however, serves as a guide to potential opportunities for future work. It does not dilute the relevance of the current findings, which can inform researchers, policy makers, and practitioners.

Notes

1 The author wishes to acknowledge the valuable feedback given by senior practitioners Choo Yee Kwan, Kasinathan Kasipillai, and Stephen Louis Silva. All errors remain the author's sole responsibility.

2 Eric H. Y. Koh is Senior Lecturer at the Department of Finance and Banking, Faculty of Business and Accountancy, University of Malaya, Malaysia.

References

Accenture. (2015a). *Accenture 2015 Global Risk Management Study: Capital Markets Report: Paths to Prosperity*. Retrieved from https://www.accenture.com/t20150806T154453Z__w__/us-en/_acnmedia/Accenture/Conversion-Assets/DotCom/Documents/Global/PDF/Dualpub_13/Accenture-2015-Global-Risk-Management-Study-Capital-Markets-Report.pdfla=en

Accenture. (2015b). *Accenture 2015 Global Risk Management Study: North American Banking Report: Paths to Prosperity: Choose Risk and Return*. Retrieved from https://www.accenture.com/us-en/global-risk-management-research-2015-banking-north-america

AuYong, H.-N. (2014). *Risk Management in Malaysian Commercial Banks*. Retrieved from www.researchgate.net/publication/269106029

Babbie, E. (2010). *The Practice of Social Research*. Wadsworth, UK and Belmont, CA: Cengage.

BAE Systems. (2016). *Managing the Risks of Cryptocurrency*. Retrieved from www.baesystems.com/en/cybersecurity/download-csai/resource/uploadFile/1434578764839

Bank Negara Malaysia. (2013). *Risk Governance*. Kuala Lumpur: Bank Negara Malaysia.

Bank Negara Malaysia. (2017). *Stress Testing Policy Document*. Kuala Lumpur: Bank Negara Malaysia.

Basel Committee on Banking Supervision. (2009). *Principles for Sound Stress Testing Practices and Supervision*. Basel: Bank for International Settlements.

Basel Committee on Banking Supervision. (2017). *Consultative Document Sound Practices: Implications of Fintech Developments for Banks and Bank Supervisors*. Retrieved from https://www.bis.org/bcbs/publ/d415.pdf

Bector, R., Herbolzheimer, C., Melis, S., and Parisi, R. (2015). Cyber-risk management: Why hackers could cause the next global crisis. *Oliver Wyman Risk Journal*, *5*, 13–17.

Bessis, J. (2015). *Risk Management in Banking*. Chichester, UK: John Wiley.

CIMB. (2016). *Annual Report 2015*. Retrieved from https://www.cimb.com/content/dam/cimbgroup/pdf-files/annual-reports/annual-report-2015-1.pdf

Clarke, P. (2015, April 28). *Six Facts about Working for JPMorgan Now*. Retrieved from https://news.efinancialcareers.com/my-en/210390/six-facts-about-working-for-j-p-morgan-now/

COSO. (2004). *Enterprise Risk Management: Integrated Framework*. Retrieved from https://www.coso.org/Documents/COSO-ERM-Executive-Summary.pdf

COSO. (2017). *Enterprise Risk Management: Integrating with Strategy and Performance: Executive Summary*. Retrieved from https://www.coso.org/Documents/2017-COSO-ERM-Integrating-with-Strategy-and-Performance-Executive-Summary.pdf

Cunningham, A. (2017, September 11). *World's Safest Banks 2017: A Measure of Safety*. Retrieved from www.gfmag.com/magazine/november-2017/worlds-safest-banks-2017

Daisley, M., Howard-Jones, D., and Naylor, L. (2014). Incentivizing risk managers. *Oliver Wyman Risk Journal*, *4*, 73–77.

Deloitte. (2013). *Exploring Strategic Risk*. Retrieved from https://www2.deloitte.com/content/dam/Deloitte/global/Documents/Governance-Risk-Compliance/dttl-grc-exploring-strategic-risk.pdf

Deloitte. (2016). *Information Technology Risks in Financial Services: What Board Members Need to Know: And Do*. Retrieved from https://www2.deloitte.com/content/dam/Deloitte/global/Documents/Risk/gx-ccg-information-technology-risk-in-fs.pdf

Deloitte University Press. (2017). *Global Risk Management Survey* (10th ed.). Retrieved from https://www2.deloitte.com/insights/us/en/topics/risk-management/global-risk-management-survey.html

Deutsche Bank. (2015). *Annual Report 2014*. Retrieved from www.db.com/ir/en/download/Deutsche_Bank_Annual_Report_2014_entire.pdf

Deutsche Bank. (2016). *Annual Report 2015*. Retrieved from www.db.com/ir/en/download/Deutsche_Bank_Annual_Report_2015.pdf

Deutsche Bank. (2017). *Annual Report 2016*. Retrieved from www.db.com/ir/en/download/Deutsche_Bank_Annual_Report_2016.pdf

Engler, H. (2016, May 13). *How JPMorgan Is Tackling the Culture Question: From Denial to Commitment*. Retrieved from http://tabbforum.com/opinions/how-jpmorgan-is-tackling-the-culture-question-from-denial-to-commitment

Engler, H. (2017, May 17). *Managing Data on Conduct, Culture a Common Challenge For US Banks*. Retrieved from http://tabbforum.com/opinions/bank-culture-reform-managing-data-on-conduct-culture-a-common-challenge-for-us-banks

Ernst and Young. (2014). *Risk Management is Changing: Act Now*. Retrieved from http://www.ey.com/Publication/vwLUAssets/ey-risk-management-is-changing-act-now/$FILE/ey-risk-management-is-changing.pdf

Financial Conduct Authority. (2018, February 5). Retrieved from www.fca.org.uk/firms/5-conduct-questions-feedback/question-1-conduct-risk-identification

Flood, J. (2009). Reviewed work(s): Fool's gold: How unrestrained greed corrupted a dream, shattered global markets and unleashed a catastrophe by Gillian Tett. *Journal of Law and Society*, *36*(4), 579–584.

Fraser, J., and Simkins, B. (2010). Enterprise risk management: An introduction and overview. In J. Fraser and B. Simkins (Eds.), *Enterprise Risk Management: Today's Leading Research and Best Practices for Tomorrow's Executives* (pp. 3–17). Hoboken, NJ: John Wiley & Son.

Friedman, S. (2016). *Taking Cyber Risk Management to the Next Level*. Deloitte University Press. Retrieved from https://www2.deloitte.com/content/dam/Deloitte/

au/Documents/risk/deloitte-au-risk-dup-taking-cyber-risk-management-next-level-030816.pdf

Global Finance. (2015). *Global Finance Names the World's 50 Safest Banks 2015*. Retrieved from www.gfmag.com/media/press-releases/global-finance-names-worlds-50-safest-banks-2015

Global Finance. (2016). *Press Release: The World's 50 Safest Banks 2016*. Retrieved from www.gfmag.com/media/press-releases/the-worlds-50-safest-banks-2016

Härle, P., Havas, A., Kremer, A., Rona, D., and Samandari, H. (2015). *The Future of Bank Risk Management*. McKinsey & Company. Retrieved from https://www.mckinsey.com/~/media/mckinsey/dotcom/client_service/risk/pdfs/the_future_of_bank_risk_management.ashx

Hida, E., and Leake, J. (2017). *The Future of Risk in Financial Services*. Deloitte Touche Tohmatsu. Retrieved from https://www2.deloitte.com/content/dam/Deloitte/global/Documents/Financial-Services/gx-global-RA-Future-of-Risk-POV.pdf

Hong Leong Bank. (2002). *Annual Report 2001*. Retrieved from https://www.hlb.com.my/content/dam/hlb/my/docs/pdf/About-Us/Investor-Relations/annual-quaterly-reports/2001/Annual-Report/Hong%20Leong%20Bank%20Annual%20Report%202001.pdf

Hsieh, H.-F., and Shannon, S. (2005). Three approaches to qualitative content analysis. *Qualitative Healthcare Research*, *15*(9), 1277–1288.

Imeson, M. (2015). Breaking bad banking and the rise of conduct risk. *The Banker*. Retrieved from http://www.thebanker.com/Banking-Regulation-Risk/Regulation/Breaking-bad-banking-and-the-rise-of-conduct-risk?ct=true

ISO. (2018). *ISO31000 Risk Management*. Retrieved from https://www.iso.org/iso-31000-risk-management.html

Ivell, T., and Jain, V. (2014). Managing operational risk. *Oliver Wyman Risk Journal*, *4*, 78–81.

Jackson, P. (2015). *Rethinking Risk Management*. Ernst & Young Global. Retrieved from http://www.ey.com/Publication/vwLUAssets/EY-rethinking-risk-management/$FILE/EY rethinking risk management.pdf

JPMorgan Chase & Co. (2005). *Annual Report 2004*. Retrieved from www.jpmorganchase.com/corporate/investor-relations/document/2004_AR_JPM.pdf

JPMorgan Chase & Co. (2015). *Annual Report 2014*. Retrieved from www.jpmorganchase.com/corporate/investor-relations/document/JPMC-2014-Annual Report.pdf

JPMorgan Chase & Co. (2016). *Annual Report 2015*. Retrieved from www.jpmorganchase.com/corporate/investor-relations/document/2015-annualreport.pdf

JPMorgan Chase & Co. (2017a). *Annual Report 2016*. Retrieved from www.jpmorganchase.com/corporate/investor-relations/document/2016-annualreport.pdf

JPMorgan Chase & Co. (2017b). *Environmental Social and Governance Report 2016*. Retrieved from https://www.jpmorganchase.com/corporate/Corporate-Responsibility/document/jpmc-cr-esg-report-2016.pdf

JPMorgan Chase & Co. (2017c). *Resolution Plan Public Filing*. Retrieved from https://www.jpmorganchase.com/corporate/investor-relations/document/resolution-plan-2017.pdf

Kaplan, R., and Mikes, A. (2012, June). *Managing Risks: A New Framework*. Harvard Business Review. Retrieved from https://hbr.org/2012/06/managing-risks-a-new-framework

Karanja, E. (2017). Does the hiring of chief risk officers align with the COSO/ISO enterprise risk management frameworks? *International Journal of Accounting & Information Management, 25*(3), 274–295.

Karanja, E., and Rosso, M. (2017). The Chief Risk Officer: A study of roles and responsibilities. *Risk Management*. Retrieved from DOI 10.1057/s41283-017-0014-z

Kloman, H. (2010). A brief history of risk management. In J.A. Fraser (Ed.), *Enterprise Risk Management: Today's Leading Research and Best Practices for Tomorrow's Executives*. Hoboken, NJ: John Wiley & Sons.

Koh, E., Avvari, M., and Tan, K. (2016). An integrated framework for competency development: Perspectives of risk managers in banks. *Service Business, 10*, 581–602.

KPMG. (2013). *Developing a Strong Risk Appetite Program: Challenges and Solutions*. Retrieved from https://assets.kpmg.com/content/dam/kpmg/pdf/2013/11/risk-appetite-v2.pdf

Lam, J. (2014). *Enterprise Risk Management: From Incentives to Controls* (2nd ed.). Hoboken, NJ: John Wiley & Sons.

Lascelles, D., and Patel, K. (2015). *Banking Banana Skins 2015*. PwC. Retrieved from https://www.pwc.com/jg/en/publications/banking-banana-skins-2015.pdf

Lim, C., Woods, M., Humphrey, C., and Seow, J. (2017). The paradoxes of risk management in the banking sector. *The British Accounting Review, 49*, 75–90.

Maybank. (2001). *Annual Report 2001*. Retrieved from http://www.maybank.com/iwov-resources/corporate_new/document/my/en/pdf/annual-report/2001/Maybank_Annual_Report_2001.pdf

Maybank. (2002, August 5). *New Maybank Group Management Members*. Retrieved from www.maybank2u.com.my/mbb_info/m2u/public/personalDetail04.do?channelId=Personal&cntTypeId=0&cntKey=AU02.08.05&programId=AU02.02-ArchiveNews&newsCatId=/mbb/AU-AboutUs/AU02-Newsroom/2002/08&chCatId=/mbb/Personal

Maybank. (2011). *Annual Report 2011*. Retrieved from http://www.maybank.com/iwov-resources/corporate/document/my/en/pdf/annual-report/2011/20110909_Maybank_Annual_Report_2011.pdf

Maybank. (2012). *Annual Report 2012*. Retrieved from http://www.maybank.com/iwov-resources/corporate_new/document/my/en/pdf/annual-report/2013/Maybank_AR2012-Corporate.pdf

Meurant, L. (2014). *Financial Crime Compliance: The Case for an Industrywide Approach*. American Banker. Retrieved from https://www.americanbanker.com/opinion/financial-crime-compliance-the-case-for-an-industrywide-approach

Portilla, A., Vazquez, J., Herreis, H., Pancaldi, L., Rowshankish, K., and Samandari, H. (2017). *The Future of Risk Management in the Digital Era*. The Institute of International Finance and McKinsey & Co. Retrieved from https://www.iif.com/

system/files/32370132_the_future_of_risk_management_in_the_digital_era_-_iif_and_mckinsey.pdf

Powell, R. (2017). New perspectives on bank risk in Malaysia. *Cogent Economics & Finance*, *5*(1), 1–15.

Public Bank. (2013). *Annual Report 2012*. Retrieved from https://www.publicbankgroup.com/CMSPages/GetFile.aspx?guid=89e6f4fa-178c-4bd4-87a0-ab9c36a72337

PwC. (2015a). *Enhancing Business Resilience: Transforming Cyber Risk Management through the Role of the Chief Risk Officer (CRO)*. Retrieved from https://www.pwc.com/gx/en/financial-services/pdf/fs-enhancing-business-resilience.pdf

PwC. (2015b, December). *Financial Services Industry: Continuous Model Monitoring*. Retrieved from https://www.pwc.com/gx/en/financial-services/pdf/fs-model-monitoring.pdf

Risk Management Association. (2018). *Who We Are*. Retrieved from www.rmahq.org/who-we-are/

Risk.net. (2012). *Bank Risk Manager of the Year: JPMorgan*. Retrieved from www.risk.net/awards/2133994/bank-risk-manager-year-jp-morgan

Scheer, D. (2018, February 2). Deutsche Bank fined $70 million for trying to rig benchmark rate. *Bloomberg Markets*. Bloomberg Markets. Retrieved from www.bloomberg.com/news/articles/2018-02-02/deutsche-bank-fined-70-million-for-trying-to-rig-benchmark-rate

Shuhidan, S., Hamidi, S., and Saleh, I. (2017). Perceived risk towards mobile banking: A case study of Malaysia young adulthood. In *International Research and Innovation Summit*. Melaka. IOP Publishing IOP Conf. Series: Materials Science and Engineering 226 (2017) 012115 doi:10.1088/1757-899X/226/1/012115

Stylianides, G., Dawson, S., and Moseley, J. (2015). *Stand Out for the Right Reasons: Facing the Future of Risk*. PwC. Retrieved from https://www.pwc.se/sv/pdf-reports/facing-the-future-of-risk.pdf

Togok, S., Isa, C., and Zainuddin, S. (2016). Enterprise risk management adoption in Malaysia: A disclosure approach. *Asian Journal of Business and Accounting*, *9*(1), 83–104.

Treanor, J. (2017, January 31). Deutsche Bank fined $630m over Russia money laundering claims. *The Guardian*. Retrieved from www.theguardian.com/business/2017/jan/31/deutsche-bank-fined-630m-over-russia-money-laundering-claims

Undheim, T. (2014). Why banks fear Bitcoin. Retrieved from http://fortune.com/2014/11/20/why-banks-fear-bitcoin/

Waslo, R., Lewis, T., Hajj, R., and Carton, R. (2017). *Industry 4.0 and Cybersecurity: Managing Risk in an Age of Connected Production*. Deloitte University Press. Retrieved from https://www2.deloitte.com/insights/us/en/focus/industry-4-0/cybersecurity-managing-risk-in-age-of-connected-production.html

Index

Note: Page numbers in *italics* indicate figures and page numbers in **bold** indicate tables on the corresponding page.

For Product Safety Concerns and Information please contact our EU representative GPSR@taylorandfrancis.com
Taylor & Francis Verlag GmbH, Kaufingerstraße 24, 80331 München, Germany

www.ingramcontent.com/pod-product-compliance
Lightning Source LLC
Chambersburg PA
CBHW060740150926
51501CB00003B/53
* 9 7 8 1 1 3 8 5 4 5 7 7 9 *